BLESSED

ARE THE

POOR

McDougal & Associates

Servants of Christ and Stewards of the Mysteries of God

BLESSED
ARE THE
POOR

*My Life and Teachings
Until Now*

BY

GANI CORUÑA

Published by:

McDougal & Associates
18896 Greenwell Springs Road
Greenwell Springs, Louisiana 70739
www.ThePublishedWord.com

McDougal & Associates is an organization dedicated to the spreading
of the Gospel of Jesus Christ to as many people as possible in the
shortest time possible.

ISBN 978-1-940461-37-3

Printed on demand in the US, the UK, and Australia
For Worldwide Distribution

DEDICATION

I dedicate this book:

To my beloved wife, Liling Cortes Coruña, who stood by me and did not leave me when I was poor.

To our children, Norman, Noemi, Gabriel (Garry), Joseph and Atty. Gani (Jay jay) Coruña.

To the memory of Erik Gunnar Eriksson and his wife Karin, Founders of Tentmission and Star of Hope in Sweden, who trusted us as partners of Star of Hope mission and work in the Philippines.

To the Eriksson siblings, Lennart, Maria and Ulrika, who continue to advance the work and legacy of their parents, the Star of Hope International mission around the world.

ACKNOWLEDGMENTS

I must acknowledge the impact of these individuals upon my life and ministry:

Rev. Harold McDougal, Founder of Christ to the Philippines and our father in the faith, whose missionary life inspired and encouraged us to continually serve our Lord Jesus Christ until now. He helped edit this book through his technical and literary expertise.

Rev. Robert (Bobby) Robinson and his wife Rita, who were kind and gracious enough to restore me as Pastor of Murphy Pentecostal Church after I came back from the United States.

All the American missionaries and families who served under Christ to the Philippines here in our country

CONTENTS

INTRODUCTION

In many ways, my life has been like a fairy tale, and at times I have had to shake my head to be sure I was not dreaming. When I tell stories from my childhood and youth, my own children sometimes can hardly believe them. But it's all true, and it's all a testimony to the greatness of God.

You see, were it not for God and His love for me, I don't know where I would be today. As a person, I was a terrible failure, so that I even contemplated ending my own life. It had so little meaning. I had been so terribly stupid, and I couldn't see how to remedy the mess I had created. Then I met Jesus, and that changed everything. Since that day, my life has not only made sense; it has been wonderfully fulfilling. And, best of all, I have been able to serve the Lord and tell others of His love. What could be more wonderful?

Here, for the first time in print, is my story, followed by selected photos of our family and work and then teachings the Lord has given me in recent years for the benefit of others. I pray that the book will be a blessing to many.

Since I have wonderful friends on several continents, I have attempted to use terms that are universally understood. For the few Tagalog words I have used, see the glossary at the end of the book,

Gani Coruña

11

He raises the poor from the dust
And lifts the beggar from the ash heap,
To set them among princes
And make them inherit the throne of glory.
                                    1 Samuel 2:8

PART I

MY LIFE UNTIL NOW

CHAPTER 1

POOR GANI!

I was born poor, very poor, the eldest of nine siblings. Three of us were born in Iloilo City on the island of Panay, but when we were still quite small, Nanay (our mother), decided that she'd had enough of Tatay's drinking, so she took us far away, back to the remote farm of her parents in the southern part of the island of Mindanao.

Their barrio, called New Iloilo, was near the border of North and South Cotabato, not far from the towns of Tantangan, North Cotabato, and Marbel (now Koronadal City, South Cotabato. My grandparents had immigrated there before World War II, since, during the American occupation of the Philippines, Mindanao was opened to settlement by people from Luzon and the Visayas. My grandparents, like everyone else in the barrio, were rice farmers. That's what the citizens of New Iloilo did.

The sides and floors of our Lolo's house were made of bamboo, and the roof was covered with the cogon grass that was plentiful in the area. Because of the animals roaming the fields, the house was elevated, and we had to climb a bamboo ladder to gain access to it.

Eventually Tatay followed us to Cotabato. He loved our mother, and so he did his best to become a farmer. This was hard for him, because by trade he was a barber.

15

While living there in North Cotabato, I started school. I had to walk two kilometers to get there and two kilometers to get back home, and I had no shoes. Most of us went to school (and everywhere else) barefooted in those days.

Our classes lasted the whole day, and so Nanay prepared a simple lunch of rice and dried fish with a slice of ripe tomato for us to take wrapped in a banana leaf.

I finished at the top of my elementary grade that year, and my parents were so proud of me that they bought me a pair of rubber shoes to wear to the awards ceremony. They were a high-cut local version of the Converse Chuck Taylor style. Because I was not accustomed to wearing shoes, they hurt my feet so bad that I never wore them again.

Tatay was just not cut out for the life of a farmer, so eventually he moved us to General Santos City (then called Dadiangas), near the very bottom of the island. Now we had a "house" of our own, and this became the only house we remembered.

In our new hometown, Tatay found work as a barber, and Nanay also worked as a *lavandera* (she washed clothes for other people), but our family was growing very quickly, and neither of them earned much, so we lived in a rickety shanty they rented in a squatter's colony, and we were packed in like sardines when the whole family slept together in one room during the night.

Squatting is a very common practice in our overcrowded cities, and it involves putting up makeshift housing on someone else's land. The actual owners live elsewhere, and there is no one there to protect their rights. Although squatters can be evicted (and sometime are), the housing situation is so critical in our country that officials often look the other way. It is surprising how many children grow up in these circumstances. Government statistics for the year 2007, for example, show that more than half a million families were living in this way. Since our families are big, that involves many millions of individuals.

There are so many squatters in our country that the government has come up with a special (and very polite) term for them. They are officially called *informal settlers*. Whatever you want to call it, squatters are among the poorest of the poor.

There was another bedroom in the house we rented in General Santos City, but it was rented by another family. Aside from the bedroom, where all eleven of us slept, there was one other room, a small dining area. Our dinner plates were made of porcelain-coated tin, and we didn't have a single fork or spoon in the house. We didn't need them because we ate with our hands, as is the Filipino custom.

There was a kitchen of sorts that occupied part of the dining room area, where our meals were prepared. It consisted of some concrete blocks with two steel bars stretched between them on which the pots were set over a wood fire. We shared this kitchen with the other family. The wood for the cooking fire had to be purchased in a nearby market.

The walls of this house were actually constructed of our cheap local concrete blocks that we call "hollow blocks," and this was somewhat unusual for squatters, but the roof was just made of that same cogon grass that was abundant in the surrounding fields, and anyone was free to collect it.

There was no electricity in the house and no running water. For light at night, we used a kerosene lantern, and fortunately there was a free flowing spring nearby. That was where we got our drinking and cooking water, that was where we washed our clothes, and that was where we took a bath. Our outside toilet was a hole in the ground with two planks stretched across it to stand on when we squatted over it.

Our bedroom furniture consisted of a homemade bamboo bed (that was full of bedbugs). The dining room table was also made of bamboo, so as we grew and needed more space, it doubled as a bed at night.

When I was ten until my early teens, Nanay had the habit of sending me to the barber shop to ask Tatay for money to buy food for the family. I remember waiting sometimes a very long while for him to give me some money, but eventually he would say there just wasn't any, and I would go home empty handed.

Sometimes it was understandable. There were not many people going to barber shops in those days because the Beatles were suddenly popular, and young people didn't want to have their hair cut anymore. It was a very bad time for barbers. On occasion I remember shivering with hunger while waiting and that eventually Tatay borrowed some money from his fellow barber, and we were able to eat that night.

That experience with hunger compelled me to look for work at an early age and earn money anyway I could, to help my parents feed our large and growing family. I started working as a shoeshine boy in my early teens. I worked as a helper on a construction site and as a port laborer, carrying heavy sacks of rice or corn. I also worked as helper to a house painter. Later, I worked at the fish port in General Santos City.

Despite the fact that I had to work and help out with the sustenance of our family, I still had a strong determination to continue my studies. Despite our poverty, I had dreams and aspirations, lots of them. I dreamed of having my own house, a car, a good-paying job and a beautiful wife. Someday I would have them all.

At one point, I wanted to be a lawyer and/or a politician. I also wanted to travel and see the world, and I knew that education was my bridge to a brighter and better future. So I worked hard at my studies.

POOR GANI!

I had a very funny experience during my high school days. Early in the morning, I would work at the fish port and then rush home to get ready for school. On one occasion, I was so rushed that I forgot to take a bath and went to class as I was. My classmates shunned me that day because I smelled so fishy. By working around the fish every day, I had grown accustomed to the smell, so that it no longer bothered me, but it turned them off.

As with a majority of Filipinos, we were born Catholic, but I don't ever remember our parents taking us to church, reading to us from the Bible or saying a prayer in our home. There was no Bible in our humble home, not even any of the usual religious artifacts. So we had no spiritual roots.

Although we were poor in a material sense, we were rich in another way — rich in languages. Like many Filipinos, we grew up speaking a mix of Philippine dialects — Ilongo, Cebuano and Tagalog — and English. This was to be important for the future.

CHAPTER 2

MY SWEET LILING

Through hard work and scholarship, I was able to finish my high school as the class valedictorian. Besides taking that top honor, I had another prize: the prettiest coed in the campus (Cecilia Cortes, whom everyone called Liling) became my girlfriend. We fell head over heels in love.

Like many young people, we experimented once too often with sex, and before long Liling became pregnant. Despite her bulging stomach, she was able to march and graduate. Before we even graduated, Liling become my wife. When I asked her why she had chosen me, when, in fact, I was poor and she had many other good-looking suitors to choose from, she answered me, "I don't like stupid guys." That sounded good to me. In time, however, she had reason to regret her decision.

It had not been easy on her to marry me in the first place. Her parents were very devout Catholics, her mother the President of the Catholic Women's League there in town, and we were nothing. Liling's family was very upset about all of this. They'd had such high hopes for her, and now she was marrying a nobody. They told her she was a fool and tried to convince her not to do it.

When she insisted that she loved me and wanted to be my wife, they arranged a mock marriage ceremony to be performed by a friend of theirs who was a judge. I didn't know until much later that he had not signed the official papers, and Liling's parents hadn't either. They were hoping she would still change her mind. When she didn't, they arranged for us to be officially married in the Catholic church. We moved in with my parents, and I started trying to find work as a house painter to support us.

Liling hated our life among the squatters. She hated the bedbugs, she hated the fact that my brothers were constantly trying to peek at our intimate moments, and she hated the fact that Tatay sometimes came home drunk. One day she confided this to her mother, and her family allowed us to move to an upstairs apartment they owned.

Our young married life was further complicated by the fact that sometimes I found work, and sometimes I didn't. So, life was hard for us. Then our first child was born, a son we named Norman, and that complicated life even more. How could we care for a family when the economy was so bad in that place?

We struggled on for a while, but about a year after Norman was born things were so bad that we decided to move to Manila. Liling's brother was there and had landed a good job as an announcer at a radio station. Surely we could find greener pastures in that huge city.

We were able to rent an apartment in the same building as Liling's brother and his wife in Del Monte, Quezon City (many don't realize that our capital city is Quezon City, not Manila). Of course, today, these and many other adjoining cities are one vast metroplex. We lived on the lower level of the apartment complex, and they lived on the second floor.

Finding a job in the capital city area proved to be much more difficult that we had imagined. I tried working as an encyclopaedia salesman, but I didn't do well at that. Although I had learned how to paint houses in Mindanao at a young age and worked some in General Santos City at it, I was unable to find work painting now. Suddenly, life was very tough in this new atmosphere.

Then, late one night, while I was walking in an area known as Kamuning, someone shot at me. Fortunately, I was not hit, but Liling and I were both shaken by this experience.

Eventually, I landed a job as a chemical salesman, and I began to do better. Unfortunately, money has its own special temptations, and I was soon to fall prey to one of them.

One of my cousins was living in the area, and we spent some time together. One evening he took me with him to a local gambling den, and I saw a very interesting game for the first time. It involved a spinning wheel, with alternating red and white spaces and two white balls. Anyone who wanted to could bet on what color the balls would land on after the spinning stopped, and if they had guessed right and both balls landed on the same space, they received as much as they had wagered. This looked like fun to me, and the idea of winning money without having to work for it was very appealing, so I decided to try my luck.

When my turn came, I placed my bet, chose my color ... and I won. I cannot describe the rush of excitement that went through me in that moment. We had struggled so to get enough money just to exist from day to day, and now I was winning more in a few minutes than I could earn in many days of working. Wow!

I put the money I had just won down and tried it again, and I won a second time. Wow! This was easy, and I had a gift for it. I put all of my earnings back on the table and made another bet, giddy with excitement. We could finally be rich and have all the things our hearts desired!

You can imagine what happened next. I lost, and I kept on losing. I lost so much that when it finally came time to go home, I was broke. I had gambled away my entire month's salary.

I couldn't believe what had just happened. We had been doing so well, and now this. I had believed that I was doing something to help us, to give us a better future, and now the future looked dimmer than ever. My head was spinning, as I tried to figure out how I could tell my lovely wife that we had no money to pay the rent, that I had gambled it all away. By the time I got home, I had made up my mind to lie to her and tell her that I had been robbed. How could I tell her that I had been so stupid as to lose all of our hard-won earnings?

Liling could not believe our bad luck. How would we buy food for the weeks ahead? How would we get milk for the baby? I tried to console her, telling her not to worry, that I would borrow some money from my boss. But then things got worse instead of better.

I was able to borrow from my boss, but then I did something even more stupid. I went back to the gambling place, certain that I could set things right, and I lost again and again. In all I lost three month's salary.

Now I could no longer invent enough lies to cover my losses, and Liling lost all patience with me and moved in with her brother and his family. Part of her motivation was that my own mother had told her that if I proved to be a problem for her, she should separate from me before we had any more children. She didn't want Liling to suffer as she had with many children she was unable to care for properly. Unfortunately for me, Liling took Nanay's advice. My story-book marriage was over, and it was all my fault!

CHAPTER 3

EVERYTHING WAS LOST

There are no words to describe how sad I was in that moment. I had caught a break in life and things had been going so well, and now, in a moment of foolishness, everything was lost, and I had no one to blame but myself. How could I have been so stupid? And what should I do now?

Within moments, it became clear to me that I had very few choices. I would have to go back to Mindanao and somehow sort out my life. But even as I boarded a ship at the Manila pier for Mindanao, all sorts of thoughts swirled through my mind. Should I go to Zamboanga City and join a smuggling ring to raise some quick cash to try to convince my beloved family to come back to me? Of should I just call it quits and take my life at sea? Perhaps when the ship was out in deep water, I could plunge overboard at night when no one was looking, and that would end it all. I was desperate and confused. It was at this terrible low point in my life that something very wonderful happened.

Before the boat could sail, I met two young ladies who had come on board. They were distributing Gospel tracts to those around them, and they looked peculiar compared to other ladies. They wore long dresses, and they had rather old-fashioned hairdos.

As good fortune would have it, they were seated just across from my cot.

Before long these young ladies handed me one of their tracts, and I said, "What is this?" They quickly explained to me the message of the Gospel and told me that if I would repent of my sins, I could be forgiven by God and receive Jesus into my heart and thus, be "saved." I wasn't sure what "saved" was, but they went on to say that God was willing to help me solve my problems, and I liked the sound of that. Could this be the very reason I was on board this ship? Did God have this planned all along?

I told them a few of my problems, but not what I had been contemplating doing about them. Before we finished our conversation, they asked me if they could pray with me, and when I agreed, they led me in a sinner's prayer. I felt this prayer deeply and wept as we prayed, and then I felt a sudden release from the bondage of sin and all its heavy burdens. I was free! It was a miracle.

It was only later that I learned the names of those two ladies: Emma Querubin and her companion Lily. I now owed them a very deep debt of gratitude.

The ship's departure was delayed because more cargo had to be loaded, and I saw a white woman approaching. She was an American and was traveling with Emma and Lily, and they introduced her to me as Sister [1] Pattie Chappell. She was, they said, their team leader.

Pattie Chappell was very happy to hear what had happened to me, and we rejoiced together. I told her my story and asked her what she thought I should do now. She felt that I should get off the ship and go back with her to their mission headquarters in Murphy, Quezon City. Why should I go to Mindanao, when my

---

1. All of the missionaries of CTTP, both foreign and domestic, when addressing each other, used the respectful terms "Brother" or "Sister."

wife and child were there in the metropolitan Manila area, commonly known as Metro Manila?

I did as she suggested. I wasn't sure what lay in store for me, but I liked the spirit of these people and felt that they could really help me to turn my life around. What did I have to lose?

CHAPTER 4

MY INTRODUCTION TO THE WORK OF CTTP

Who were these people? And why was I there meeting them? They were all working with a group calling itself Christ to the Philippines. I was to learn that Christ to the Philippines had formed as a result of the vision of an American man from West Virginia named Harold McDougal and his Filipino co-workers.

Brother Harold had met a Filipino businessman in a campmeeting in Virginia some years before, and he had then felt a call to join this man in his work in our country. Harold had thought it would be for a short time only, because another American missionary was scheduled to come out and take his place after sixty days, and he wanted to go on to India. As it turned out, he was in the Philippines for many years — the next seven years to be exact.

In their early years, the McDougals (joined a year later by the Robinson family), had a burden for unreached places. They would organize crusades in outlying areas that had no Charismatic church and start one. Country people themselves, their message was very simple, and it appealed to the simple people of our countryside. Most importantly, they asked God to do miracles of healing in each of their meetings, and it was these miracles that convinced many of the validity of their message. Soon churches were established in parts of several Luzon provinces, including Rizal, Bulacan, Nueva Ecija, Nueva Vizcaya, Laguna and Maria Aurora and many areas of the Bicol region.

Then something changed dramatically in this ministry. Through a series of events known as the Spiritual Fiesta, which were televised in many major cities of our country, the missionaries of Christ to the Philippines, along with their growing number of Filipino associates, began receiving invitations from many of the Catholic institutions, especially those related to priests and nuns, to come and teach on prayer and the infilling of the Holy Spirit.

At the same time, our government opened the schools to the CTTP teams to go in and teach classroom by classroom, pray with the teachers and students, and place a Gospel of John in their hands. During summer recesses, the CTTP teams would go to the tribal areas of our country, preach and distribute Gospel portions in the languages of those minorities. Over a two-year period, more than 1.25 million gospels were placed in this way. The Asian edition of *Time* magazine reported that a thousand priests and nuns and ten thousand Catholic lay people had been filled with the Spirit in the Philippines during this same period.

Because of the success of this ministry and its acceptance in high places, there were now weekly live telecasts from the main church in Quezon City and ten radio programs a day over popular stations around the nation, as well as the crusades being conducted in schools, on military bases and in selected convents and monasteries. This mission was clearly making a difference in our country, and my excitement grew as I learned about these things.

When Pattie Chappell got me to the mission house in Murphy, the first thing she did was tell me to get a haircut. I had adopted the long-haired style of the day, and the CTTP ministers and students all wore their hair short. Then she introduced me to some of the other missionaries.

The missionaries of CTTP were all very happy for me. They loved my testimony and were so happy about what had happened on that ship at the Manila pier. For them, this was what it was all about. A soul saved made their many sacrifices worth it all.

In the process of our discussions, they encouraged me to believe that Liling would want me back. I wasn't sure of that. She had been so disappointed in me for what I had done. I wondered if she would ever have me again. They suggested that I call her immediately and tell her what had happened to me. I wasn't sure that I could even put it all into words, or if she would believe a word I was saying.

With their encouragement, I called anyway, and was very pleased that Liling did not totally dismiss what I was saying as another lie. She seemed to believe me, and we spoke of meeting in a few days and talking it all over.

Next, I was taken to a communal living quarters a couple of blocks away from the mission house, and there I met many of the students who were currently preparing themselves through the CTTP Missionary Training Center for a future ministry.

This center was based on an interesting concept: Although Bible teachings were given every day and Bible verses were memorized, more emphasis was placed on prayer and fasting, learning to hear the voice of God and learning to be sensitive to the Holy Spirt's guidance. The students and teachers prayed together every morning for an hour and again in the afternoon. Several evenings a week the students were required to attend services in the church. Often there were special speakers from other countries who would challenge them.

Other subjects that were taught, with the goal in mind of producing missionaries to eventually go out to other nations, were: English Improvement, Geography (especially Asian), and some History of the Asian nations.

Once this classroom training was complete, the students were then formed into teams and sent out to begin what was called their Field Training period. During the coming months, they would work with a more experienced team leader and would do any type of ministry that opened to them. They were expected to preach, teach or testify when called upon, and then pray with those who responded to their message. Their audience might be school students, military recruits, or the members of local churches.

Those students who successfully completed these two training periods were then considered for more serious missionary work in the surrounding nations. In that same two year period, Filipinos ministered in more than twenty other nations, and that was just the beginning.

CHAPTER 5

RECONCILIATION WITH LILING

Within a few days of staying there in the men's dorm on 13th Avenue, I had made some wonderful new friends. Two of those friends, Luciano Cariaga from Bicol and Bert Rigodon from the Manila area, kept encouraging me to believe for a complete reconciliation with Liling, and they even offered to accompany me to go see her. Because of how I had lied to her about the lost money, I was afraid that she would not want me back, but together we went to see what could be done.

The atmosphere was a little chilly at first, but we explained to Liling what had happened to me, and she listened carefully. I had two things to give her that I hoped might make the difference. (1) I had an envelope with some money given by the CTTP missionaries in return for some painting I had done around the mission house. This would help the family situation, and (2) I had the phone number of the CTTP mission house. If Liling didn't believe me, maybe one of the missionaries could convince her that I had really changed.

Liling agreed to call the CTTP office, and it was Rita Robinson who answered the phone that day. I owe Sister Rita so much because she was able to convince my lovely wife, whom I had hurt so badly, that I was a new man and also persuaded her that the right thing to do would be to reconcile with me, without fear that I would do the same things again.

Thank God, and to Him be the glory, Liling agreed. What a happy day it was for both of us when we were reunited! Our love was suddenly rekindled and burned brighter than ever before. I was happy to have my family back, and Liling was happy to have a new husband. And, of course, we were both happy to know Jesus and to have a new hope for the future.

CHAPTER 6

SOME TRYING TIMES

What should we do now? After such a dramatic change, could we just go back to living our lives in the normal way? That didn't seem possible. We had learned so much in such a short time and were both excited about what these CTTP young people were doing for God and our country. More importantly, it was not just about Gani, Liling and Norman any longer. There was another Person in our lives. We had agreed to make Jesus not only our Savior, but also our Lord. What did *He* want for us in the days ahead? What was *His* will for our lives? If we could find His will, our new friends assured us, things would go well for us. If not, we might slip back to the old way of life and lose everything.

Liling and I talked it over, and we agreed that because God had been so gracious and merciful to us, as a matter of gratitude, we should both serve Him the rest of our lives. That decision made, we enrolled in the Bible training program of Christ to the Philippines.

In former years, CTTP had a nice Bible school building they had built in the mountains of Sampaloc, Tanay, Rizal, but a very strong typhoon had damaged that building so severely that it had been abandoned for the time being.

33

The headquarters of Christ to the Philippines was located at No. 10 11th Avenue, in Cubao, Quezon City. This was also the missionary house where the American missionaries lived. Adjacent to the mission house was a church that the missionaries had built. The entrance to that church was on 12th Avenue. This became our classroom for our Bible school training, and we went there each weekday for prayer and study.

The housing for the rest of us was in a rented building two blocks away on 13th Avenue. It had been erected originally as an old theater building, but it had not been used for many years, so the missionaries rented it, and that was where all the students, as well as any workers who happened to be home at the time, slept and ate. That was where I had stayed while waiting to be reunited with Liling and where I had met so many wonderful friends. The place wasn't so bad for single men, but for Liling, it was a nightmare.

The building itself was a World War II Quonset hut. For those who may be unfamiliar with this type of building, Dictionary.com states:

> *Quonset hut:* a semicylindrical metal shelter having end walls, usually serving as a barracks, storage shed, or the like, developed for the U.S. military forces from the British Nissen hut at Quonset Naval Base in Rhode Island.

In other words, these were prefab metal buildings used by the military for all kinds of activities, and after the war many were made available to the public through surplus. In fact, Quonset huts are still in use in many parts of the world today. In the U.S., they are especially popular for farm use.

This particular Quonset hut was very big, but it had been abandoned for many years, and, as noted, had never been used for housing, only as a theater. The Philippine military from nearby Camp Crame sent engineers to help tear out the old balcony risers, to create a level area where beds could be placed for the single ladies and to make more bathroom facilities. So all the ladies stayed upstairs on the balcony, nearer to the metal roof, and it was very hot up there.

The downstairs had few dividers. It had been left as a large open space where people could sit and watch movies. It, too, had relatively few windows, and because of the metal roof, during the heat of the day, it was nearly unbearable in there.

Quonset huts were never very practical in the Philippines for everyday use without air-conditioning precisely because: (1) Those metal roofs collected heat, and (2) There were few windows to provide ventilation. This particular building had no air-conditioning at all, so those of us who stayed there suffered a lot.

One large room to the side with a sloping floor was filled with homemade bunk beds, and that's where the single men stayed. Other areas of the downstairs were partitioned off to make places for married couples and our cook and her young daughter.

At the start, Liling and I were assigned to a tiny room with a small bed just outside the Quonset hut. That sagging spring bed was about three feet wide and six feet long, and the three of us had to sleep on it together. One day Brother Harold came by, took a peep inside our room, took pity on us, and moved us inside the Quonset hut to that partitioned area, together with another family. Now, at least, we had a larger plywood bed.

This life was particularly difficult for Liling. She was not used to such conditions. Her father worked in a bank as a property assessor, and they owned their own home. They were not rich, but they were also not poor. She suffered a lot in those days.

The food for all those who lived in the 13th Street building was prepared en masse and was often not to everyone's liking. At times, it was limited, so that we were forced to fast, whether we wanted to or not.

Another difficult part of that time was that we were being taught to "live by faith," which meant that we had to trust God completely to supply everything we needed, even our basic daily needs. That was more than difficult for those who had no source of income. It was a trying time for.

Because Liling was pregnant, she experienced certain cravings. At one point, she was craving what we called "banana que" (cooked banana on a stick) and Coca-cola. It was nothing unusual for a pregnant women to have such a craving, but we did not even have a single peso to buy what she wanted, and that bothered her. I suggested that we kneel down together and pray about it, and we did.

After prayer, we went out of the room (because it was so hot in there), and as we stepped out the door, lo and behold, there was a ₱5 (Philippine peso) note at our doorstep. We had no idea who had put it there, but I ran out, crossed the street, and bought some banana on a stick and a 1.5 liter bottle of cold Coke. Liling was delighted with that answered prayer, and so was I. We were learning to trust for everything.

CHAPTER 7

OUR FIELD TRAINING

When we had successfully completed our classroom training, we were then sent to do our field work. We were to go to schools, churches, military establishments and anywhere else we found an opening and preach the Gospel of our Lord Jesus Christ. We also gave out and distributed Gospel portions (the Gospel of John) after preaching to the people and the students. We were mostly preaching in Catholic schools and colleges.

Since Liling had Norman to care for, she was exempted from this part of the training at first. I was blessed to be sent to Indonesia with Brother Bert Colosaga, and we followed the same pattern of ministry there for about a month.

Back home, I was sent out with Luciano to the Bicol region. Luciano had a wonderful singing voice, and so often he would sing and have me preach. One of his favorite songs that he sang quite often during that time, was "I've got my one-way ticket to the sky." Together we ministered in schools and churches wherever we went. It was a very rewarding time.

Back at the dorm in Quezon City, an interesting thing happened. While I waited on my next assignment, it began to seem as if the three of us — Liling, Norman and I — had no room to move aound. Our very narrow space seemed to be closing in on us. This was so opressive that at one point, we began contemplating quitting the ministry and going back to Mindanao. Our situation was just too difficult.

While we were thinking on these things, Norman suddenly experienced an epileptic seizure. It was so severe that we could not bear to look at him. He was trembling and gnashing his teeth, and his eyeballs had turned white.

I picked Norman up and raised him to the Lord in prayer. "Here," I said, "just take our son, but please don't let him suffer anymore."

Then I had a second thought: "If you don't want to take him, Lord, then heal him, and we promise to serve You the rest of our lives." Instantly, Norman's epileptic seizure ceased, and that was the last one he ever had. Oh, our God is so wonderful and awesome! Glory to His name! Hallelujah! We were committed to serving Him — in the good times and also the bad.

We did go to Mindanao, but not in defeat as we had been thinking. Instead, we went for ministry. We visited and ministered in many schools, mostly Catholic schools, like the Notre Dame colleges. So that we could move about better, we left Norman with Liling's parents in Polomolok, a town near General Santos City. It was a wonderfully fruitful time.

After going back to Manila, next Liling and I were sent out together again, this time to Mindanao the province of Zambales. Our first mission stop was the town of Botolan. Besides our bus ticket, we had just been given ₱100.00 pocket money (about US $12.50). It was night when we arrived there, and we had no contact and nowhere to sleep. Liling was pregnant again, and I was carrying a box of Gospel portions. Norman, who was now two, tagged along behind us as best he could.

Before we could get very far, we were intercepted by some local policemen, wanting to know who we were and why we were in their town. When we told them that we were missionaries, they were very kind and offered to help us. They took us to a Catholic convent where nuns accommodated us and took good care of us. They gave us a place to sleep and fed us well.

We gave those sisters our personal testimonies, and they allowed us to preach in their schools, as well as in their churches. It was a wonderful opportunity. What a great miracle that the way was opened for us to penetrate the Catholic institutions. For so long, they had been closed to any non-Catholic preachers. It was a new day, and we were being able to experience it and participate in it.

Chapter 8

Demons at Our Window

We had a phenomenal experience while staying in a Methodist pastoral house there in Botolan. We were still half asleep toward the middle of the night when we suddenly heard the moaning and crying of a woman. There was also a clanking sound of chains, as if someone was dragging fetters. At the same time, we heard the incessant howling of dogs outside (the moon was very bright that night). Then Liling saw a woman at the window. But how could anyone be out there when we were staying on the second floor of the house?

It was hot, so Liling had gotten up to open the window, and there was the woman smiling in at her and attempting to reach out and touch her very pregnant tummy. She seemed to have an elastic hand. Liling froze and was unable to move, but in her mind she kept rebuking the woman, saying, "In the name of Jesus!"

When I heard Liling, who was obviously struggling with something, I came wide awake and immediately jumped to my feet. I had goose bumps all over me. Something very strange was going on.

Our faith in God was strong, and I rebuked that evil spirit with a loud voice, saying, "In the name of Jesus, go away, you evil spirit!" Those phenomena all stopped, and we were able to sleep soundly the rest of the night and every night after that. Hallelujah! Our God is powerful! Glory to His name!

The next day, while having breakfast in another house with our hostess, a lady pastor, she told us that she had heard some commotion during the night. We told her our experience. She said she had deliberately put us in that house, which, she said, was haunted, so that she could test us to see if we were true servants of God. Now she was sure that we were, and this gave us many more open doors in churches and schools, to preach the Gospel of our Lord Jesus Christ.

We hated to leave Botolan, but Liling was due to deliver our second child in about three weeks time, so we felt we had to get back to Manila.

CHAPTER 9

A MIRACULOUS DELIVERY

We didn't have money to buy the things we would need for the baby, and we wondered what we would do, but God was faithful. He moved on the heart of the wife of one of our members, Attorney Saquing, and she gave Liling ₱1,000.00 (a large sum of money at the time) and said it was for the baby's needs. She said the Lord had spoken to her in a dream several times to give the money. He is faithful to supply all our needs.

Liling also had a dream, but her dream was not a pleasant one. She dreamed that she died during the delivery. Two other sisters among our ministry companions — Necitas Besas and Zenaida Antivo — also dreamed that Liling died during her delivery. Because of this, we were both frightened, and I prayed earnestly that the Lord would save both Liling and the child.

For Liling's part, the dream was so real that she told me who she wanted me to marry — Nora Genoves, a sister who could sing well. I was determined that Liling would live. I took her to Labor Hospital in Quezon City on her due date. It was (and still is) a hospital that served the poor. Several hours passed, and she was still in the delivery room. The doctor had done several things to induce labor, but for some reason, the baby was still not coming. Liling later told me that the doctors had begun shaking their heads, indicating that there was no hope for her or the child. They believed both would die.

I was called into the delivery room, and I saw with my own eyes the doctors shaking their heads. I wept, thinking that both Liling and the child were already dead. "There is nothing more we can do," the doctors told me, and they warned Liling not to go to sleep.

I immediately laid one hand on Liling's stomach and, with the other hand raised, I said with a loud voice, "In the name of Jesus, come out!" To the amazement of everyone in the delivery room — including me — the child came out. It was a girl, and she was alive.

"Oh, my God!" one of the doctors said, "Only the name of Jesus was the remedy."

The baby looked purple, and the doctors concluded that if her birth had been delayed much longer, she surely would have died. She lived, and we named her Noemi.

Praise the Lord! Hallelujah! There is power in the name of Jesus!

CHAPTER 10

BEGINNING PASTORAL WORK

Before the American missionaries left the Philippines and went back to the U.S., they asked me to succeed Rev. Robbie Ridenour as pastor of the local church, known as Murphy Pentecostal Church. I reluctantly accepted this appointment, because, quite honestly, it was a very big challenge for me. There were several things that gave me pause.

For one, our training had been in evangelism, not in the pastoral ministry, and most of our experience since then had been in evangelism, not in pastoral work. I could see that this was something very different.

Another thing that bothered me was that most of the members of the church at that time were Bible school students. They were accustomed to having an American pastor them and were not happy to have me instead. Many of them, in fact, no longer attended the church services after I took over.

In part I believe that these young people were influenced by one man and his family. For some reason I never fully understood, they were hostile to me. This complicated matters because he was one of the elders of the mission and a teacher at the Bible school. In time, I came to suspect that he saw me as competition. Personally I had never considered the ministry to be a competition. I was learning about the politics of the church.

I think this animosity toward me all started when Filipino missionaries were sent out to the Asian nations, and I was one of those chosen to go (and he was not). Apparently he had been expecting to become pastor of the church, and when I was chosen instead, he never got over it.

I tried to ignore the hostilities and concentrate on how to increase the membership of the congregation beyond the students of the Bible school. Fortunately for our family, there was one American couple still working with CTTP. They were Rev. Fred Jensen and his wife Darlene. Brother Fred loved evangelism, so their work with CTTP was doing evangelistic crusades throughout the country. They now did a crusade in the Murphy area of Quezon City. The meetings were held at an open area of the water tower near Camp Aguinaldo. During several nights of crusade, many people were saved and gave their lives to our Lord Jesus Christ. I diligently did the follow-up of these converts, through visitation and Bible studies, and some new members came in as a result.

I also did my own personal evangelistic crusades in West Crame, San Juan, Metro Manila. Scores of people gave their lives to Jesus as a result of those evangelistic efforts. Through follow-up and Bible studies, these new converts to our Lord now made up the bulk of the membership of our church.

Most of these people were poor, and they lived in the squatters colony. Their dwellings were made of light materials and were rather skimpy, and they didn't own the land their houses sat on, so they could not give much to the church. Nevertheless I patiently continued to work with perseverance among these people, nurturing them into spiritual maturity in Christ.

Because we had poor members, the church itself was poor, and I, as the pastor of a poor church, was also poor (as far as finances were concerned). Although we lived free of rent at the back of the church, we had a very limited income, and our family, now with three children, was growing. The early teachings we had received on faith in God and the concept of living by faith strengthened and sustained us during these difficult times and caused us to remain faithful to the ministry.

During one of the annual national conventions of Christ to the Philippines, attended by bonafide members of the mission from throughout the country, stretching from Mindanao to Luzon, I was elected as a member of the Board. Besides the yearly election of the national officers, there was always a wonderful festive mood of fellowship among the members at these gatherings, with food and spiritual encouragement through the messages of the special speakers.

As a board member, one of the resolutions that I personally worked hard on was the purchase of the properties of the mission office in Murphy and the Bible school in Tanay, Rizal. For some reason, I was strongly opposed on this by most of the other members of the board. Sister Etta Hampton, one of the few remaining American missionaries, was also a member of the board at the time, and she backed me up. Eventually the resolution was adopted.

Looking back now, I am glad that I proposed these enactments, for in my opinion, this helped to stabilize and strengthen the mission work of Christ to the Philippines for the future.

CHAPTER 11

OBEDIENCE IS BETTER THAN SACRIFICE

Things seemed to be going well for a while, but eventually the daily grind of the ministry coupled with the difficulty of providing for a growing family discouraged me, and I decided to try my luck in the United States. We knew others who had gone there and done well, and I thought it might be worth a try.

Bobby Robinson, the missionary in charge at the time, reluctantly granted me leave and covered for me as pastor of the church, and Liling and the children (now three with the birth of Gabriel, whom we called Garry) stayed in a small room at the back of the mission house.

My entry into the United States was made possible through the kindness of David and Mary Clever, pastors from Maryland, and they were generous enough to let me stay in their home while I was there. Her brother, Lauren Yost, helped me set up a speaking itinerary in a number of small churches.

Like most people, I was drawn to the U.S. by the talk of greener pastures. I had heard many say that the United States was a land of promise and opportunity. I needed something to happen because Liling and I had been struggling to meet the basic needs of our growing family. My weekly support from the church at the time

47

was only ₱150.00. We were not complaining, because we knew that wouldn't help things, but sometimes I had been forced to do some moonlighting in order to augment our meagre income.

True enough, when I arrived in the U.S., I found it to be a land of opportunities, especially for those who are diligent and industrious. I had it good there, and, in fact, was having "the time of my life." I said to myself, "This is it! Hallelujah! Praise God!" I looked forward to being able to bring the whole family over as soon as possible.

Our American brothers and sisters in the Lord were very good to me. Their kindness and generosity touched me deeply. After I preached or gave my personal testimony, people came to shake my hand, and there was often money between our palms. They called it a Pentecostal handshake. We call it *aDollar pa*.

I was especially blessed to meet Pastors Jim and Betty Perry. What a sweet couple! They always treated me for lunch at Ponderosa Steakhouse. They have supported us and been partners in our ministry ever since.

Before too long, one of my pastor friends said to me, "Your English is not all that bad; if you would like, you can work as my assistant. Then, through the church, you can petition for visas for your family to come over." Wow! That sounded wonderful! I was thanking God and rejoicing in the answer to my prayers.

I was in the U.S. for nearly six month when one day a still small voice spoke to me that I should go back to the Philippines. I really struggled with this idea. My flesh was happy right where I was. I tried to shake off this feeling, but I couldn't. When I sought confirmation from my pastor friend, he confirmed it. "Yes," he said, "you should go back to the Philippines because your people need you there." That was not what I wanted to hear, but it was what I needed to hear. I knew he was right and knew what I must do.

OBEDIENCE IS BETTER THAN SACRIFICE

Being a committed servant of God and of our Lord Jesus Christ, I obeyed and came back to the Philippines. This was to be a serious turning point in our lives. As God's Word teaches us, obedience is better than sacrifice. [2]

---

2. See 1 Samuel 15:22

CHAPTER 12

THE SWEDISH CONNECTION

Not long after I obeyed the Lord and came back to the Philippines I received a phone call from a man who said that he wanted to visit our church that Sunday. His name was Sigvard Wallenberg, and he said that he was with two other men, and they were all three from Sweden. He was working with a ministry known as Star of Hope International, and according to him, the Lord had spoken to him to come to Asia in the midst of his busy schedule in Scandinavia.

While the men were in Thailand, the Lord told him to go to the Philippines, but he told the Lord that he didn't have any contacts there. The Lord told him to go anyway.

The men were staying at the Holiday Inn in Manila. After they had prayed together, they decided to go down to get a cup of coffee. Inside the lift, someone had posted a church directory, and that was where they got our phone number.

I went to their hotel early Sunday morning to pick them up. I was amazed to see that they were all big tall blonds. Sigvard, the biggest and tallest of them, asked me, "Where is your car, Brother?"

I said, "I don't have a car. I'm just a poor pastor."

"Then you'd better go find us a taxi!" he said.

I found a taxi, but it was small (most Filipinos are small in stature), so he couldn't get into it. While trying to squeeze himself in, he ripped his pants. Yes, it was a pretty funny scene. Sigvard went back to his room to change his pants, and I went in search of a larger taxi.

When we finally arrived at the church, the Swedes were surprised: (1) To see how small it was, and (2) To see what happy people we had. As is our custom, everyone was clapping their hands and joyfully singing to the Lord.

When Sigvard sat down, he smashed one of our plywood chairs flat, but they enjoyed their time with us that day. Before they left, they said they had been touched by the plight of some of the small children they had seen in the streets who looked undernourished to them and promised to help us through a feeding program. They also promised to help me buy a used car. Because many people promise help and never come through, I didn't take their offers very seriously. I was surprised a month later when I opened my box at the post office to find a check for US $3,000.00 and a note saying, "Get yourself a used car, Brother!"

Praise the Lord! Hallelujah! I knew this had to be from God!

From that day on, Sigvard and his friends in Sweden began to help us with a number of wonderful projects. Later, Liling and I were curious about how all of this had started. We decided to go by the Holiday Inn where the men had stayed because we wanted to see that "church directory" they told us about and find out how we had gotten on it. Strangely, no church directory could be found.

We asked several of the hotel employees about the church directory, and they answered, "What church directory?" One man said, "I have been working here for ten years, and I have not seen that church directory you are talking about. We don't post a church directory here in this hotel!"

So who put it there? Many simply say, "Surely God works in mysterious ways." I call it Divine Providence. This was but the beginning of our partnership with Star of Hope in Sweden for the work of the Lord in the Philippines.

CHAPTER 13

THE TRANSITION

I took Sigvard and introduced him to our organizational director, but Sigvard told me that he was not led to work with the organization, only with me personally. This caused some confusion in the organization, because of the funds that were coming in for various projects, and I was eventually asked to vacate my position as pastor of the Murphy Church. I assured the members that a new pastor would be coming to take my place, and Liling and I began to pray about where we were to move. In the end, we were led to move to West Crame in San Juan, another part of Metro Manila, and start another church.

Although I was no longer pastor of the church in Murphy, I was still a member of the organizational board, for I could be replaced only after a vote of all of the pastors in our annual gathering. During this interim period, I started assisting some other pastors in the group with financial aid from Sweden. This, too, was misunderstood. I had not wanted to draw them away from the group, only to be a blessing to them financially. This was all very sad for us, because these were our brothers and sisters, and this was the place where we had been saved and then trained for ministry. Our hearts were heavy.

When the annual meeting of the organization was eventually held that year, I suppose I thought the result was a foregone conclusion. Liling and I had accepted an invitation from Sigvard to visit him in Sweden during that time. We visited Swedish churches and raised funds for the work in the Philippines. As anticipated, I was replaced on the CTTP national board, and our time with the mother organization thus came to a close. Our partnership with Sigvard and his Swedish friends at Star of Hope was strong, so the future looked bright.

CHAPTER 14

THE BUILDING

Backed up by Star of Hope in Sweden (which we soon registered in the Philippines), we found and rented a large old house in West Crame with three bedrooms and a garage. We held our first service in the garage, and there were seven people in attendance.

West Crame was another poor area. I continued with my working strategy, trusting the Lord to give us souls in this new place. Through the coming months and years, the church membership grew into a fairly sizable congregation, and we continued rejoicing in the Lord for His faithfulness, especially in meeting our needs financially for the rent of the house and church.

After we had rented that house for three years, the owner decided to sell. The property consisted of more or less 720 square meters. We were the first ones he informed about his intention to sell. The selling price, he said, was about two million pesos. He said he would give us three months to raise those funds. If we were not able to buy it, he would sell it to another interested buyer. It was a large amount of money for us to raise in such a short a time, but we started working on it.

In the first Sunday service after that, I announced our intention to raise funds to purchase the church property, and I challenged the members of the congregation concerning the urgency of this endeavour.

I had a Rolex watch that I had acquired through some of my moonlighting activities, trying to keep the family afloat financially. I valued that watch highly, but now I took it off, held it up and told the congregation: "My Rolex watch is worth fifty thousand pesos. I am going to put this in the offering plate today to raise funds to buy the church property. I will redeem the watch with ₱50,000 cash to get the fund started. If you are willing, you can take off your valuables — like watches, gold earrings, necklaces or other jewelry — and put them in the offering plate. Put a cash value on them and then redeem your valuables with cash, just like I plan to do." There was a wonderful response. Everyone took off something of value — a watch, earrings, a necklace and other jewelry — and put them in the offering plate. In this way, we were able to raise more than ₱100,000 that first Sunday.

In the next services, no one came with jewelry on. But those first acts represented our seed money, and the Lord provided the rest, so that were able to purchase the building. Then, we went on to invest ₱3,000,000 more into developing it!

Hallelujah! Glory to God!

CHAPTER 15

JOSEPH'S FORMULA FOR SUCCESS

I was searching the Bible for answers during one of our periods of financial difficulty, and the story of Joseph found in the book of Genesis inspired me. How wonderfully God lifted him up out of his difficulty. The drama of Joseph's life was so amazing that I wept as I read it again. I was not weeping out of sadness for our own situation, but, rather, because I felt that I could identify with the man in his trying situations. He suffered a lot, but then, very suddenly God caused him to graduate from his school of trials and gave him an amazing transition to a life which could be summed up as "From the prison to the palace."

The interpretation of Pharaoh's dream and the solution that Joseph suggested to Pharaoh seemed to jump off of the page at me that day, and I got very excited. Seven years of plenty followed by seven years of famine seemed to me to be much like the economic cycles that we all go through, as individuals and as nations. Everyone seems to experience prosperity and economic ease at least sometime in life. With businesses and other commercial endeavors, we call it a windfall. Farmers sometimes reap a "bumper crop." But there are also times when everything seems to be difficult, no matter how hard we work. Now I was seeing that, during the times of plenty (according to Joseph's economic formula for success) we have to set aside a certain percentage of our income in preparation for years of famine or economic depression. By adopting this simple economic formula, I felt that I could break the cycle of poverty in my life and get out of financial difficulty.

Even though we were living in the parsonage rent free, Liling and I decided that we would set aside a certain amount of money in savings, as if we were paying rent. As a result, financial blessings began to flow to us. Sometimes we didn't even know the people who were giving to us.

At one point, a American medical doctor appeared at our door. He said he needed someone to accompany him on a personal mission to the Visayas and Mindanao. I agreed to accompany him, and I took advantage of the visits to do some evangelism in each place. Before he went back to the States, he gave us US $1,000.00. I later learned that he was the brother of the founder of a well-known accounting firm doing business in Manila. He was Dr. Sycip, brother of Washington Sycip of Sycip, Gorres, Velayo and Company.

Then there was Pastor Jim and Betty Perry who began to send us a monthly offering of US $200.00. Eventually I had accumulated enough capital, so that I was able to do some moonlighting. For instance, I was able to buy and resell some used cars at a profit.

I began teaching this practical economic principle to the poor members of our church. Why should we buy ice from across the street to cool our drinks when we could afford to buy a refrigerator? The priority, of course, was for each family to own a home because renting consumed so much of their income. We had the same goal for ourselves.

CHAPTER 16

THE JERICHO MARCH

Liling's brother-in-law came back to the Philippines from years of working in Canada and planned to retire here. He asked me to help him find a piece of land close to Manila so that he and his wife could build a home. I agreed to help him.

In our search, we eventually came upon a subdivision we liked called Easter Heights. It was just below the American school called Faith Academy in Cainta, Rizal, close to Antipolo, a place known for its fresh breezes and lack of pollution. There was a corner lot of about 570 square meters that Liling particularly liked. There were lots of shade trees around, and it was so peaceful. How wonderful it would be to have a home there! Liling decided to claim that lot and proceeded to do a Jericho march around it. She went around it seven times proclaiming, "I claim this property in the name of Jesus!" Without her knowing it, I had been saving and setting money aside for just such an opportunity.

In the end, the brother-in-law lost interest in the land and went back to Canada. I contacted the owner and began to negotiate the price. The owner happened to be one of the Marcos boys. They were having to flee the country about that time, and so they urgently needed to liquidate their property.

59

The wife was the one transacting with me, and I got the property at barely half the current market value because the family was in such dire need for money. The next time I invited Liling to go there, I had a surprise for her. I told her, "Behold, this land is ours. I bought it." She was overjoyed. We borrowed to build our first home. Thank You, Jesus! Glory to God!

In time, we were able to acquire the adjacent lot, I borrowed again and built another house. This one was smaller than the first. Another property acquisition was a 248 square meter lot with an older bungalow house in Pasig City. We renovated the old house, and it was ready for sale.

But things were going so good that I suddenly found myself bring sucked into real estate ventures, wanting to enrich myself, and, in the process, neglecting the work of the Lord. I woke up from that financial trance and knew that I had to stop. I must concentrate on the job the Lord had given me, pastoring His flock.

We lived in one of the smaller houses, renting out the other two, and the rents paid the mortgages. In other words, those properties were self-liquidating. They are now fully paid, and our family is living a comfortable life. Thanks be to God! Glory to His name!

CHAPTER 17

STARTING A SCHOOL MINISTRY

Although we have always remained apolitical, we have also coordinated and cooperated with local government officials like the mayor of the city, when it came to social and humanitarian concerns in the area where our church was located. Besides evangelism, this has been one of our church strategies to reach out to the people of our community. At one point, I received a phone call from the then-mayor of San Juan, Joseph Estrada (who later, became our president).

Mayor Estrada said, "Pastor, I need your help. We just moved more than 600 squatter families to a resettlement area in Taytay, Rizal, and they need an elementary school there. Can you put one up? I have provided a vacant lot of about 6,500 square meters for the project."

It took me a while to answer him, and I spent that time in prayer as in consultations with other believers. The reason was that I had no prior experience in putting up or running a school. I knew that it would be a real challenge for me, but after much thought and prayer, I decided to accept the offer.

During our first visual inspection of the area, I was shocked to find that it had been a garbage dump. There was a mountain of smoking trash there, and the stench of it permeated the entire area. Other drawbacks were: there was no passable road to the place, and the area was swampy. The mayor's Toyota Land Cruiser that we used to go there got stuck in the mud halfway, so we had to get out and walk.

When we reached the resettlement area, I asked the residents there how they were able to reach the place. They said, "We use the creek and move about with a small boat that is kept nearby." The poor families who had been relocated there had already put up their skimpy shelters, but not one of them had electricity. They were living in pitiful conditions.

Once I had seen all of this, I was even more challenged to help the people to have a decent elementary school for their children to attend. Before we tried to start building the school, I asked Mayor Estrada if he could at least fill the swampy road with gravel so that we would be able to transport the needed construction materials to the site. He was gracious enough to do that.

During consultations with our Swedish partners, I was assured of funding for the school construction. In the meantime, we would have to register a new branch of Star of Hope in the Philippines, this one dedicated solely to education.

The needed funds were eventually provided by SIDA, the Swedish International Development Agency. In this way, a school for Taytay was completely funded by the people of Sweden. We called it Star of Hope Christian School.

We started with an elementary school and later were also able to put up a high school. The school population, in terms of enrollees, has grown from 300 children when we first started, to more than 2,000 at present. I have felt very blessed to be entrusted with this sort of ministry. There is no doubt in my mind that all of this favor came from our God! Hallelujah! Praise the Lord!

The motto of our school is: "Breaking the cycle of ignorance and poverty through education." Besides being a Christian school, it is also a witness to the entire community of the Gospel of our Lord Jesus Christ.

CHAPTER 18

INTERVENING IN INFANTA

In December of 2004, a devastating mudslide cascaded from the mountains of Infanta, in the province of Quezon, killing more than two thousand nearby residents. Star of Hope responded with an emergency relief operation to the mudslide victims with food, clothing, blankets, water and other relief goods. Soon afterward we received another grant from SIDA to build 300 core houses for the calamity victims.

To be able to do this, we purchased two hectares of land in Baranggay Ilog in Infanta. One hectare was allocated for those core houses and the other for an elementary school. We sensed that once we moved the families to this housing area, their children would need a school to attend. Through private contributions and donations from the people of Sweden and Norway, another school was established in Infanta. We started with grades one to three, but now we are up to grade six already, as classrooms are being added.

Looking back through the years, I have witnessed the immensely transforming impact the school has had, not only on the children, but also on their families and the community. Before we put up the school in Taytay, Rizal many of the children at the San Juan

Resettlement Site were not even attending school. They were scavengers at the nearby smoky mountain dump site. When they enrolled in our school, they were not only delivered from scavenging; many of them are now professionals in their own right and are able to help their families. The quality of the houses in the area has improved immensely.

I lobbied with the local authorities who have jurisdiction over this political subdivision to improve the road system and also to put up electrical power lines and a water system for the community. Although it has come slowly, the community where the school is located has now obtained those basic infrastructures which were so badly needed. The houses in this community now look rather presentable. In the beginning there were only 600 families, but now there are more than 6,000 families living in the community, and it is still growing. We see that the school has been a catalyst, an agent of change for the better for the children, their families and the community.

CHAPTER 19

GOD DOES MIRACLES TODAY

In 2012, Liling suddenly suffered a stroke. She was immediately rushed to the hospital and into the ICU (intensive care unit). Her right eye and mouth had collapsed, and her face looked disfigured. The doctors also found a lump in her ear, which, they said, was dangerous. She needed immediate surgery.

The operation was successful, but Liling's face remained disfigured, and the hospitalization and surgery were expensive, very expensive. The total hospital bill amounted to hundreds of thousands of pesos. God had already provided the money we would need for it (through our savings).

Although Liling was out of the hospital now, she would have to take a very expensive maintenance medication. The doctors also recommended therapy for her disfigured face and a hearing-aid for her ear.

Shortly after she came home, Liling locked herself in our bathroom one day for two hours. Worried and concerned for her, I forced opened the door. I found her there prostrate on the floor, weeping. "What happened?" I asked her.

She surprised my by replying, "Leave me alone. I'm praying to God!"

When she finally came out of the bathroom that day, her face was totally restored, and she was just as beautiful as ever.

According to Liling, while she was praying, she heard three clacks on her head: "Clack! Clack! Clack!" When she looked in the mirror, she found that her face had been restored.

She went to the ear doctor for the hearing-aid appointment, and the doctor was surprised to find that she was hearing well enough without the need of a hearing aid. He said, "Well, we do our best, and God does the rest!"

Who says that miracle days are over?

Jesus Christ is the same yesterday, today, and forever.
                                        Hebrews 13:8

He is our God who heals us, and by the stripes of Jesus we are healed. [3]Our God is powerful and wonderful! Praise God! Glory to His name!

---

3. See 1 Peter 2:24

CHAPTER 20

WITH GOD, NOTHING IS IMPOSSIBLE

After twenty years of existence, Star of Hope Christian School in Taytay had amassed a stunning testimony. Yearly enrollment had risen steadily to more than 2,000 children a year. In those twenty years, more than 77,000 children had studied in the school, and more than 12,000 have graduated from the elementary and high school.

But there was a problem: The school property (more than 6,500 square meters) was on what is called an usufruct contract with the City of San Juan that was specified to last just twenty-five years. It was to expire in 2014, and it was stipulated in the original contract that the entire property, including all the improvements, would revert to the City of San Juan at that time. What could we do?

I had asked our teachers several years before if they could think of any way we could extend our contract for another twenty-five year period. They all answered, "Impossible!"

I also asked all the parents, and they agreed, "Impossible!"

I turned to the church members and asked the same question, and they had the same answer — "Impossible!"

Oh, my, we had a triple impossibility on our hands. We needed a miracle from God. Prayer was mobilized in the church big time!

One day I visited the Mayor of San Juan City, the Honorable Guia Gomez, and prayed with her. Then we talked about what we could do for Baranggay West Crame. She told me, "You know, Pastor, I really want to help the people in West Crame, but the land is so expensive there!"

I smiled and replied, "There is a vacant and available lot of 740 square meters there. If you want it, let's swap land, since our contract with you is about to expire."

Her answer was: "Let's do it!" In this way, IMPOSSIBILITY #1 was solved!

In order for the mayor to enter into a contract for a land swap, she needed the concurrence of the twelve city councilors by way of a City Council Resolution. After about a year of public hearings and deliberations, the resolution was finally approved unanimously! IMPOSSIBILITY # 2 was solved.

Now we needed money (millions of pesos) to pay for the Crame property to be swapped with the school property. Lennart Eriksson, Maria Presson and Ulrika Kallin, the Eriksson Siblings at Star of Hope in Sweden, worked relentlessly to raise the much-needed funds. In the end, the Ek Family of Sweden, led by Lena Ek and her children, donated the money to help pay for the Crame property. IMPOSSIBILITY #3 was solved.

In this way, we not only retained possession of the school itself, but God gave us full ownership of the school property. Praise His holy name! Hallelujah! Our GOD is awesome! Is anything too hard for the Lord? No! Nothing is too hard for Him!

CHAPTER 21

GOD'S SACRIFICIAL AND GENEROUS PEOPLE

Before I close this part of the book, I must give thanks to two groups of people: (1) The missionaries who served selflessly for so many years to bring us the Gospel, and (2) The many generous people who have supported their efforts and ours.

This first group is large. As noted earlier in the book, Liling and I were converted through the evangelistic endeavors of American Missionaries who came to the Philippines in the mid-1960s. These people left the comforts and luxuries of their homes in America. Some of them even sold those homes, their cars, their valuable possessions and even their businesses to do this work. They gave everything to missions and then lived by faith in the Philippines doing the Lord's work.

These American missionaries were led by Rev. Harold McDougal. Together with his wife Diane and their children (born here), he founded the mission known as Christ to the Philippines. After a year, they were joined by Rev. Robert Robinson and his wife Rita. In the early 1970s, these two families were joined by Rev. John Chappell, III, his wife Pattie and their children, Rev. Robbie and Bonnie Ridenour and their children and Etta Hampton. Later came Lauren Yost and wife Pat, together with their children and Rev. Fred Jensen and his wife Darlene. The Jensens became national evangelists of the mission and stayed for many years traveling around the Philippines from north to south conducting evangelistic meetings even in remote villages. There were others, but these were the ones I knew personally.

These American missionaries suffered the privations of being in a foreign land, from tropical sicknesses like malaria, from natural calamities and were even sometimes destitute of the very necessities of life. But with passion, they patiently persevered and prevailed with their commitment to God.

They sacrificed their lives and suffered for Christ for the sake of the Gospel. Like Moses, they must have been motivated by something or someone who was unseen. We are forever grateful to them because of all they did. If they had decided not to leave their all in the U.S., we would have not heard the Good News of salvation through Christ. Many other Filipinos join me in thanking them.

The other group may not have spent long years here, but their sacrifice was equally important. They financed all that was done then and is being done now. I have already mentioned a few of the Americans who blessed us in this way. To me, some of the most generous and kind people in the world are the Swedish and the Norwegians. In my experience, when they give, there are no strings attached.

The most generous and kind individuals I have met in my life were Peter Ek his wife Lena and their children Lisa, Rasmus and Johanna. This Swedish family, whom I have been told, were descended from missionaries, have sponsored and paid for the schooling of hundreds of poor children whose parents could not afford to send them to school. For some of these students, the Eks continued to support them even up through college. They have done this now for more than twenty years and are still doing it today. Some of the sponsored children, therefore, are already grown-ups and have become professionals in their own right.

Peter and Lena also helped build the Star of Hope school in infanta, Quezon and gave start-up capital to some families in General Nakar, Quezon, for livelihood projects such as pig raising. They also helped build houses for their sponsored children. The most memorable of these acts of generosity was when Peter and his family took some two hundred very poor children from Payatas, West Crame and Taytay, Rizal for Christmas shopping at one of the malls in Cubao, Quezon City. I personally witnessed the joy and excitement on the fact of these children. It was their first time to go inside a mall, and they were able to freely purchase whatever they wanted: clothing, shoes, toys, school supplies, or anything else.

After the shopping, the children were treated to a meal at a local restaurant. This became an Ek family tradition, and every year poor children are treated to a Christmas shopping trip. Talk about giving the joy of Christmas to poor children! This is praiseworthy. Liling and I deeply admire this family and are trying to emulate their benevolence to the best of our capacity and in our own way. Our prayer is that God may bless every generous soul who has given in any way to make possible the work we do here every day. Their rewards await them.

CHAPTER 22

WHAT THE FUTURE HOLDS

My how the years fly by! At first, it was just Liling and myself. Then came Norman, then Noemi, then Gabriel, then Joseph (an adopted son), and finally Gani, our youngest and my namesake.

Norman grew up and married Rhoda, and they have three wonderful daughters: Micah, Jessica and Sylvia. Micah has already finished college, and the other two continue their collegiate level studies.

Noemi, the result of that miraculous birth after we had returned from our Zambales, mission, finished college and has a degree in Psychology. She is married and has a son.

Gabriel (Garry) earned a degree in Computer Science. He married Tina, and they have two daughters: Gabrielle Marie and Issabelle.

Joseph, who also earned his degree in Computer Science, is still single.

It's hard to believe, but Gani, our youngest, is now a practicing lawyer. Wow! God is so good.

Sigvard died in 2010, but our relationship with the good people of Sweden continues strong, and Star of Hope Philippines continues to bless many people.

And that's just my life until now. I am just 64 as of this wring, and the future looks bright as we move forward to serve our Lord in any way we can. My intention is to continue pastoring until I draw my final breath and to continue to expand and improve our school projects for the benefit of future generations.

To God be all the glory!

PART II

THE PHOTO SECTION

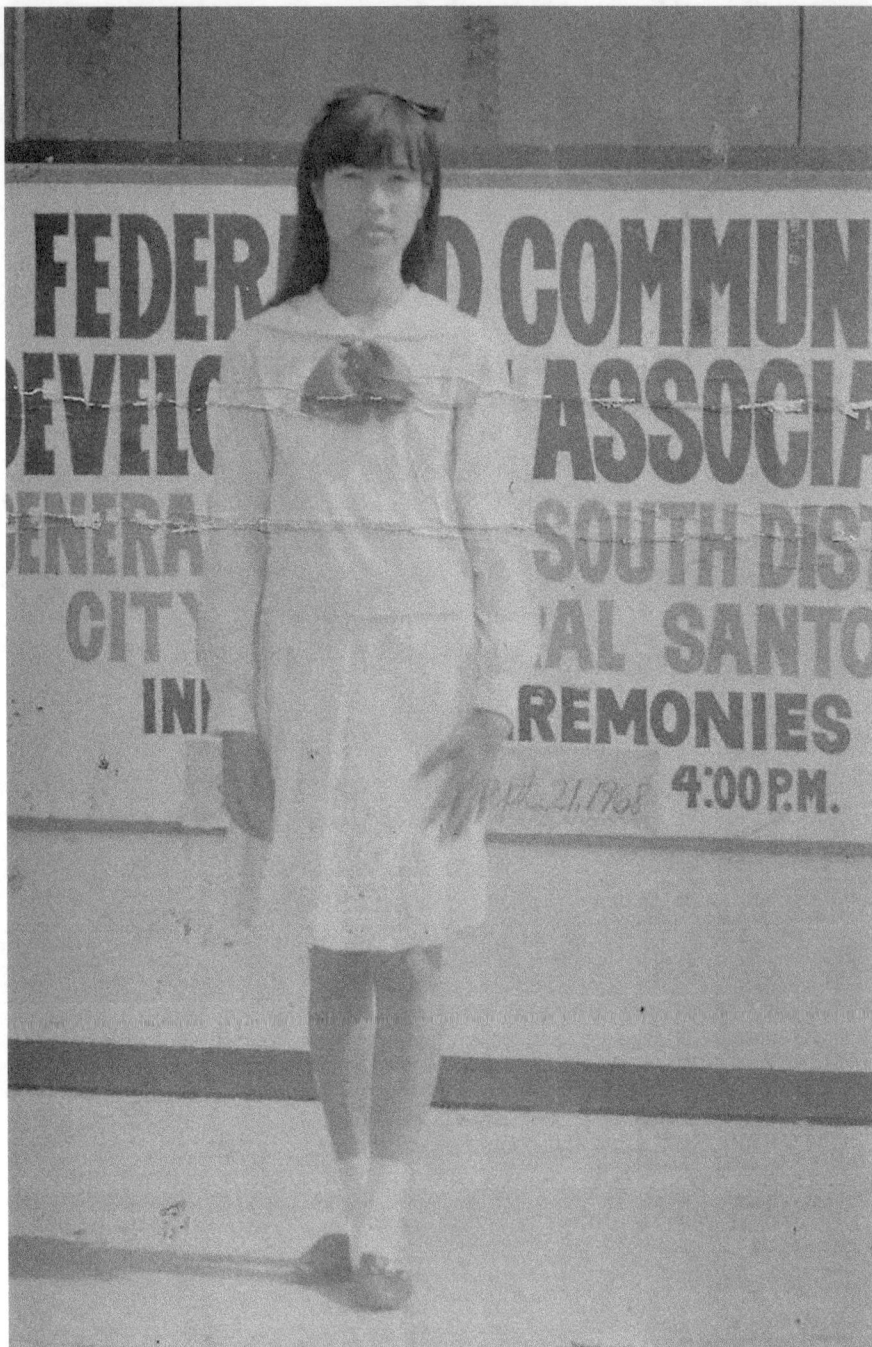

Liling as a student 1968

Liling with Norman

The three of us in 1973

Coruña Family in the Philippines

The Coruña Family in 2013

Merry Christmas & A Blessed New Year
Coruña Family 2014!

In front of the Rikstag, Sweden's seat of power

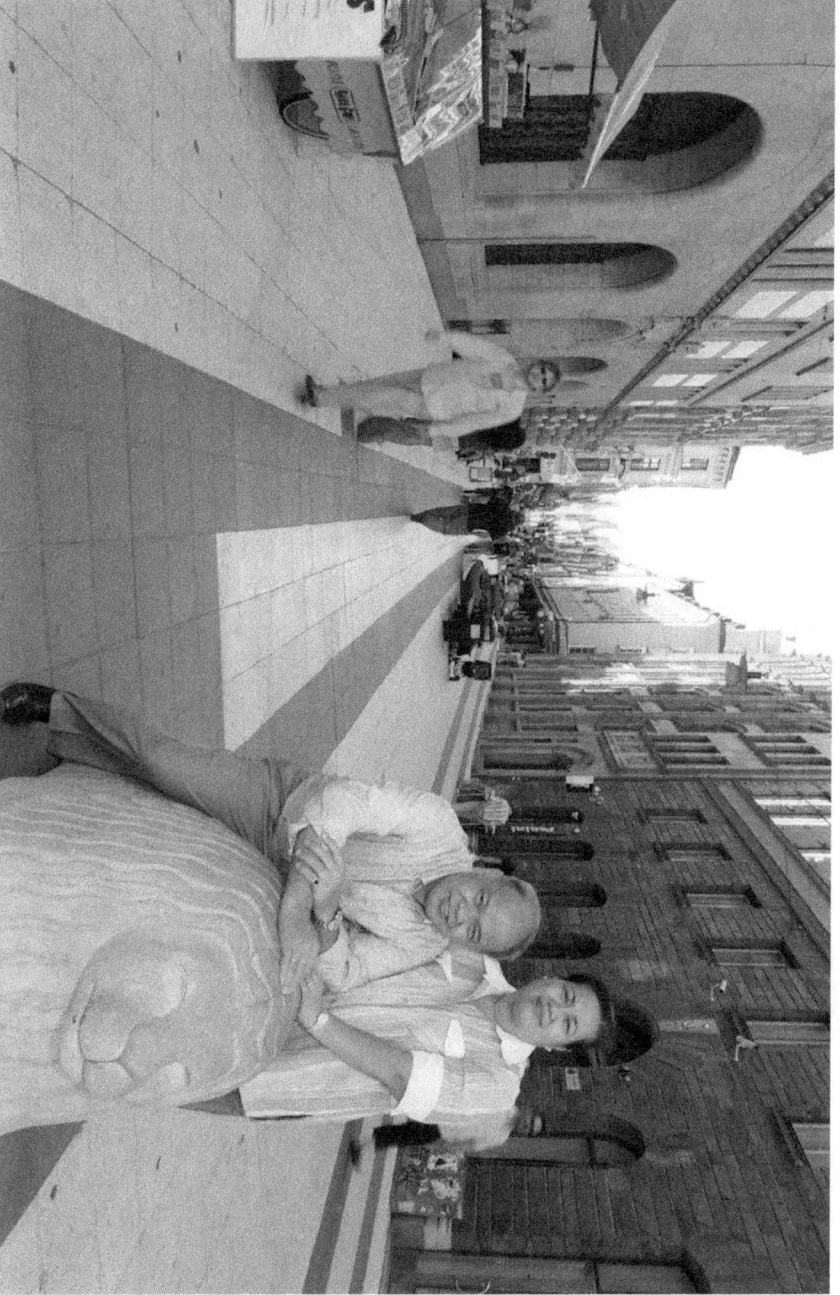

On Stockholm's famous waling street, Drotningsgatan

Our last visit to Sweden

In front of the Royal Palace, home of King Carl XVI Gustaf of Sweden

87

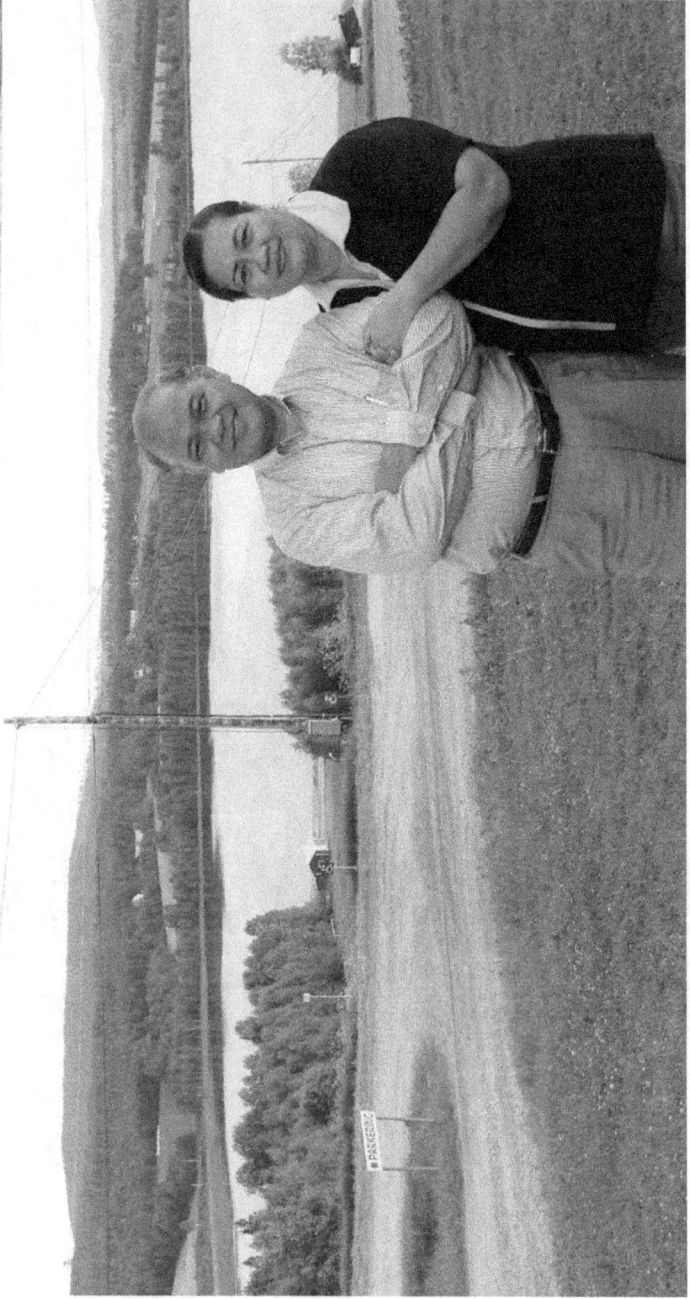

In front of the beautiful lake facing the Star of Hope headquarters building

In front of the Star of Hope headquarters in Sweden

89

The Ericksson Family

The Eircksson Siblings Grown

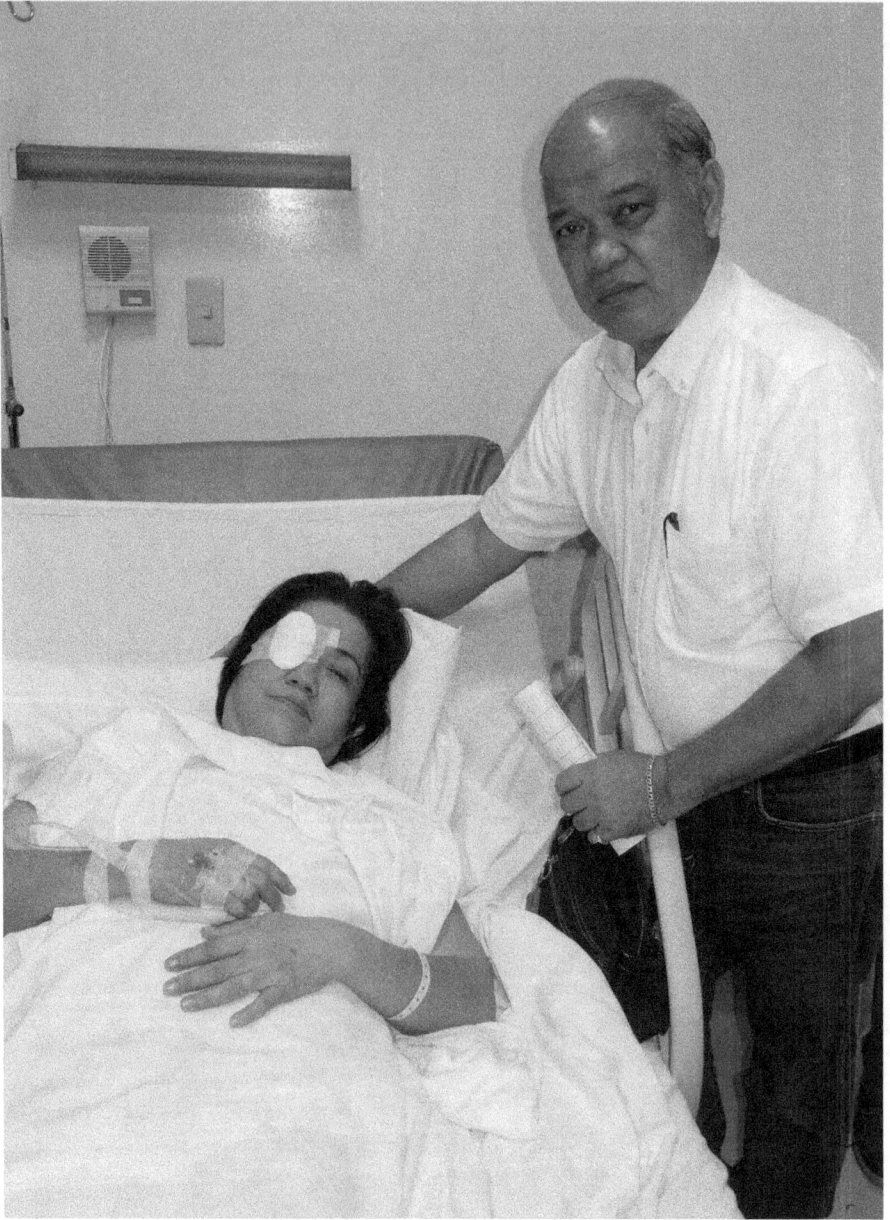

With Liling in the hospital

Our congregation at Christian Faith Church

The Taytay School

The Infanta School

The Crame school ground-breaking ceremony with VIPs holding shovels: Congressman Ronnie Zamora, City Mayor Guia Gomez and Vice-Mayor Francis Zamora

The crowded area we serve

A sample of Metro Manila's acute housing crisis

PART II

MY TEACHINGS

INTRODUCTION

What follows are some short messages the Lord has given me in recent years. They are in no particular order, and there is some overlap from one to another. Each one was intended to stand alone, so we have not bothered to remove any duplication or to combine those of a similar theme. May they be a blessing to all those who read them.

Before you begin reading, let me say that I know some of my teachings are rather unorthodox and many may disagree with them. If you have accepted the Lord Jesus Christ as your personal Savior, you are my brother, and I respect your views on these and other subjects.

Gani Coruña

WOW, WHAT AN AWESOME AND AMAZING BODY!

We are confident, I say, and willing rather to be absent from the body, and to be present with the Lord.

2 Corinthians 5:8, KJV

Proponents of the mainstream Christian belief that, at death, the soul immediately goes to Heaven use this verse, among others, to support their argument. A closer look at the text and even the context, however, reveals that it does not mention the word *death* at all. "Well, doesn't *'absent from the body'* mean death?" some argue, "And no one goes to be *'present with Lord'* [in Heaven] without undergoing death, do they?" That's true, as a general rule. But there is an exception to every rule, and I am convinced that it is the exception to this rule that Paul was contemplating here.

How could that happen? He explains it in 1 Corinthians 15 and 1 Thessalonians 4, where he describes a sudden and abrupt change that will come to those who are still alive at the time of the Rapture.

The main thrust of Paul's message here in 2 Corinthians 5 is found in the context. He was talking about two bodies, the earthly and the heavenly. These two bodies are different, and he describes the difference between them by way of an allegory. The first one he likened to a tent (the wilderness Tabernacle), and the other one to a building (the Jewish Temple). The former was temporary, and the latter was permanent. Both structures were indwelt by the presence of God and were where the ancient Israelites met and worshipped Him at the time.

For some reason, Paul said, he groaned, and he mentioned this phenomenon twice (see 2 Corinthians 5:2 and 4). This was an indication that he was in pain and/or that he was burdened. It is apparent that the multiple trials he mentioned in 2 Corinthians 4:8-10: *"troubled on every side," "perplexed," "persecuted," "cast down"* and *"bearing about in the body the dying of the Lord Jesus,"* had taken a toll on his body. At one time, he had a *"thorn in the flesh"* that he sought the Lord to remove (2 Corinthians 12:7). Was this some kind of physical health issue he suffered as a consequence of the rigors of ministry?

Perhaps you and I can identify with Paul in the many bodily infirmities we suffer, especially as we grow older. Our bodies are deteriorating, and we have many aches — headaches, toothaches, backaches and even knee aches. Sometimes (or most of the time) we have no one to blame but ourselves. We have failed to take care of our bodies through indiscriminate, reckless, careless and callous living. We have abused and misused our bodies with uncontrollable vices. Excessive drinking of alcohol, an addiction to smoking or other tobacco products or the use of illegal drugs have weakened and destroyed our body's immune system so that we are suffering from diabetes, cancer, AIDS, or some other disease. Paul asked:

> *Do you not know that you are the temple of God and that the Spirit of God dwells in you?* 2 Corinthians 3:16

102

Wow, What an Awesome and Amazing Body!

Because this is true, we must keep our bodies clean — physically and spiritually. Paul added:

If anyone defiles the temple of God, God will destroy him. For the temple of God is holy, which temple you are.

2 Corinthians 3:16

Oh, the reality and the curse of being human!

But there is good news! God has prepared a new body for us. That new body is heavenly, it is immortal (meaning that it will not die, but will live forever), it is incorruptible (meaning that it is not subject to decay and deterioration), it is powerful (not limited by time, space or the law of gravity), and it is spiritual. Wow! That sounds like a Superman. Yes, God is preparing a whole new breed of people.

In the first verse of this 2 Corinthians 5, Paul wrote:

For we know that if our earthly house of this tabernacle were dissolved, we have a building of God, an house not made with hands, eternal in the heavens.

2 Corinthians 5:1

"We know ..." How did they know? He had already told them in 1 Corinthians 15, where the subject is the resurrection. They had that assurance.

Many might say, "I want the kind of body you are writing about. Where can I get it?" It is not a matter of where, but a matter of how and when? The condition is this: Repent of your sins and accept Jesus as your personal Lord and Savior. Commit your life to Him and follow Him the rest of your days. Then you will have *"the earnest of the Spirit"* (2 Corinthians 5:5)!

YES, OBEDIENCE IS BETTER THAN SACRIFICE

And my God shall supply all your need according to His riches in glory by Christ Jesus.   Philippians 4:19

When I went to the United States that time fairly early in my ministry, my intentions were good. I was not abandoning my faith or my ministry. I felt that I was doing the responsible thing by looking for other ways to provide for my family. Surely I could find the answer I needed in the land of opportunity. The United States proved to be all that I had dreamed of and more.

Then, as I noted earlier, after I was there for less than six months, the Lord spoke to me to come back home to the Philippines. I really struggled with that decision. In the end, I asked a pastor friend to help me pray about it, and he confirmed the Lord's will for me to return.

Reluctantly, having experienced the difficulty of meeting my family's needs, I obeyed the Lord. After all, He was Lord, and surely He knew what He was doing. True to His Word, within a few years, the Lord had given us, fully paid, our own church building in West Crame, San Juan. (And the building is fully air-conditioned.) He also gave us the school ministry with its corresponding properties valued in the millions of pesos. God gave us our own home (fully paid) at Valley Golf in Cainta, Rizal, and he gave me a personal car, a Mercedes Benz E-220. It's an oldie, but it's also a goodie.

Not so long ago, Gani, our youngest son, passed his bar exams and became a full-fledged attorney. Praise God! Hallelujah! Our God is wonderful, and He is the best Employer ever.

I want to encourage pastors and other ministers who may be going through trials and difficulties, especially in meeting your basic needs. Be patient, be obedient and be faithful in your service to God. He will supply all your need according to His riches in glory by Christ Jesus! He guarantees it.

HEAVEN CAN WAIT

In My Father's house [Heaven] are many mansions; if it were not so, I would have told you. I go to prepare a place for you. And if I go and prepare a place for you, I will come again and receive you to Myself; that where I am, there you may be also.

John 14:2-3

Today there are many ministers, including theologians, who proclaim that those who have died (assuming that they are committed Christians) are already in Heaven and are in a better state than we are. This doctrine is based on a belief that the soul survives death and immediately goes to Heaven. When I asked one of the proponents of this doctrine about his definition of *death*, he answered, "Separation."

I followed this with another question: "What separates during death?"

His answer was, "The immaterial from the material."

When I asked him if he could elaborate on that, he declined to answer. What he probably meant was that at death the soul separates from the body and immediately goes to Heaven.

The big questions now is: Are there really people in Heaven now? Or could those ministers of the Gospel be mistaken? Let's find out.

The proponents of this belief cite several verses from the Bible as a basis for their doctrine. Let's just mention two of them. The first one is in Hebrews 11:5, and it alludes to something mentioned in Genesis 5:24. Hebrews 11:5 (KJV) says this:

By faith Enoch was translated that he should not see death; and was not found, because God had translated him: for before his translation he had this testimony, that he pleased God.

Genesis 5:24 says this:

And Enoch walked with God: and he was not; for God took him.

Most Bible translations of Hebrews 11:5 say that Enoch was *taken, taken away* or *taken up*. Only the Living Bible (and the New Living Translation) render the verse as to say that God took him to Heaven.

Many argue that Enoch did not die, thereby suggesting that he was somehow immortal. Is that right? Did Enoch not die? And is Enoch in Heaven now, as many claim? A careful reading of Hebrews 11 will show that Enoch indeed did die. Referring to the heroes of faith mentioned throughout this chapter, verse 13 states: *"THESE ALL DIED in faith, not having received the promises ..."* (Emphasis mine). That included Enoch, so it is an established biblical fact that Enoch died.

And the answer to the second question is: No, Enoch is not in Heaven. As a matter of fact, except for Jesus Christ, who is God, no one is in Heaven yet. To say that God took Enoch to Heaven, then, is an error. He is definitely not in heaven. His body, which decomposed and turned to dust, is still here on earth. His tomb in Iraq was destroyed by ISIS militants in recent months.

When confronted with seemingly contradictory passages in the Bible, we pastors have a responsibility to seek the guidance and spiritual discernment of the Holy Spirit. We cannot always extract the truth of a certain passage by random reading. For this reason, we have been disciplined to exegete and always consider the context in relation to the text.

Why does Hebrews 11:5 say that *"Enoch was translated that he should not see death?"* No reason is given, so we can make a conjecture relative to Enoch's situation at the time. Probably it was by reason of expediency or emergency. He did not die in the place from where he was translated, but he eventually died in the place he was translated to, as verse 13 suggests.

This word *heaven* in the Bible has three different dimensions: the first, the second and the third heaven. The first heaven is the immediate atmosphere of earth where there are clouds. The second heaven is outer space, and the third heaven (Heaven) is the abode of God, sometimes referred to as paradise, a city or a country. It is probable that Enoch was taken up to the first heaven, when he was translated by God. We can cite similar situation with the prophet Elijah (see 2 Kings 2) and with Philip in New Testament times (see Acts 8:39-40).

Another verse of the Bible that is used to teach that there are people in Heaven now is Luke 23:43:

And Jesus said to him, "Assuredly, I say to you, today you will be with Me in Paradise."

The controversy about this verse is whether the comma should come before the word *today* or after it. That simple act changes the meaning. Did the translators or the printers perhaps make a simple mistake?

This verse was quoted to me by an opposing minister, who chose to believe that the malefactor, to whom Jesus addressed these words, went to Heaven (Paradise) that very day when they both died. When I suggested that this was a future promises, he accused me of twisting the Scriptures.

It is my strong and firm conviction, as a follower of Christ, that our Christian life and beliefs are real, rational and logical, never an illusion, so I asked him this question: "Where did Jesus go that day when He died? Did He go to Paradise, together with the malefactor? He did not answer.

The Bible, however, answers this question. Jesus was taken down and buried, and He was in the tomb for the next three days and nights. He did not go to Paradise together with the malefactor that same day.

"If Jesus was in the tomb," I asked the man, was Paradise in the tomb, or was the tomb a paradise?" There was still no answer.

There is noting to indicate that the malefactor was put in the tomb together with Jesus. Jesus was buried in one tomb, and the other man was buried in another.

One of the pastors of a large Christian denomination told me that the reason he and others say that those who have died are already in Heaven is just to comfort their loved ones. I thought that was a very poor excuse. The best comfort we can give others is to tell them the truth. And what is the truth about this issue?

Because we are unable to reconcile these seemingly conflicting and contradictory passages in the Bible regarding this subject (or any subject, for that matter), we must listen to Jesus. He is the

Final Authority, and by His words men will be judged. What did Jesus say:

> *No one has ascended to heaven but He who came down from heaven, that is, the Son of Man who is in heaven.*   John 3:13

> *In My Father's house are many mansions; if it were not so, I would have told you. I go to prepare a place for you. And if I go and prepare a place for you, I will come again and receive you to Myself; that where I am, there you may be also.*   John 14:2-3

Before anyone goes to Heaven, Christ must come again, for no one goes to Heaven by himself. When Jesus returns, that's the time that He will receive those who died in Christ and the Old Testament saints, together with those who are alive in Christ who will be suddenly changed at the time of His return. This was confirmed by Paul in his first letter to the Thessalonians:

> *Brothers and sisters, we do not want you to be uninformed about those who sleep in death, so that you do not grieve like the rest of mankind, who have no hope. For we believe that Jesus died and rose again, and so we believe that God will bring with Jesus those who have fallen asleep in him. According to the Lord's word, we tell you that we who are still alive, who are left until the coming of the Lord, will certainly not precede those who have fallen asleep. For the Lord himself will come down from heaven, with a loud command, with the voice of the archangel and with the trumpet call of God, and the dead in Christ will rise first. After that, we who are still alive and are left will be caught up together [this is the Rapture] with them in the clouds to meet the Lord in the air.*

And so we will be with the Lord forever. Therefore encourage one another with these words. 1 Thessalonians 4:13-18, NIV

Personally, I find this teaching to be contrary to the Scriptures. Whereas the Bible says, *"The soul that sinneth, it shall die"* (Ezekiel 18:4), these people say that the soul survives death. Besides, the definition of *death* is "the absence of life," and to me that refers to the soul.

Death is the cessation of all vital functions, and it is the end of life (which is in the soul). So, what soul are they talking about going to Heaven when it is already dead, according to the Bible?

The proponents of this teaching, when proclaiming that the soul lives on after death and goes to Heaven immediately, are resurrecting, in effect, those dead people (souls) and sending them to Heaven by saying, "They are already in Heaven." That is an act of usurpation, for only God has that right. We cannot resurrect people (souls) and send them to Heaven ahead of God's time. Only God has the authority and the power to resurrect people (souls) and take them to Heaven, and it will be done according to His timeline, not ours. So, this is serious error.

Do I mean to say that Christians will not go to Heaven? On the contrary, it is only a matter of when and how. Yes, Heaven can wait!

I urge my fellow pastors and preachers to discard and abandon any erroneous doctrines concerning the life to come. I am convinced that the root of this doctrine goes all the way back to the Garden of Eden, where the devil had the gall to say to Eve, *"You will not surely die"* (Genesis 3:4). She believed that lie, and when one believes a lie, what do we call that? Deceived!

THE MORTALITY ISSUE OF THE HUMAN SOUL

And the LORD God formed man of the dust of the ground, and breathed into his nostrils the breath of life; and man became a living soul. Genesis 2:7

This is clear: When God formed man, He did it with dust from the ground, and then He breathed into man's nostrils the breath of life, and it was at that point that man became a living soul. Still, in mainstream Christianity, there is an issue regarding the soul of man that I find difficult to understand, and I have debated the matter with many well meaning pastors.

Despite the clear, convincing and overwhelming evidence to the contrary, one pastor insisted that man was created immortal by God even before the Fall. It was God Himself who pronounced to Adam, *"You shall surely die"* (Genesis 2:17), and yet many continue to contradict this truth and, instead, continue to concur with the line of the serpent (the devil) who lied and deceived Eve when he insisted, *"You will not surely die"* (Genesis 3:4). There is clearly a conflict here, and someone is wrong. One side of this argument is the teaching of God, and the other is the teaching of men.

Many err when they connect this soul issue to the issue of the of man. To prove to them that man indeed was created mortal even before he sinned against God, I told them, "Sin or no sin, man would have eventually died anyway because by nature he was mortal." To respond to this, they formed into two threads. The first thread challenged me to a debate on the proposition: "Was sin the cause of the death of man or not?" I was on the negative side and used Genesis 2:16-17 as the basis for my argument.

The lead debater on the opposing side opened by asking me this question: "Do you agree that sin had a consequence on Adam and Eve when they ate the fruit of the forbidden tree? "

I answered,"Yes, I do."

When my turn came to ask a question, I posed this one: "Did Adam and Eve die that same day when they disobeyed God?" He could not answer.

I asked the same question four times with no response. Finally, I said, "If you are not willing to answer the question, them I'm out of here."

Eventually he answered, and his answer was "no."

I said, "Then that's it. End of the debate! You just validated my position with your answer."

A definition of terms could be useful here:

- *soul* — life in the physical body
- *mortal* — subject to death
- *immortal* — not subject to death: deathless;
- *death* — the absence of life; the cessation of all vital functions of physical/natural life.

The Bible mentions three kinds of death: physical death, spiritual death and the second death. The mortality issue of the soul is connected with physical death. This death is not the annihilation of the soul but simply the temporary absence of life. Sometimes, in lieu of the word *death*, the Bible **actually** uses the word *sleep*. Jesus used this word (see John 11:11), as did Paul (see 1 Corinthians 11:30) and also Daniel (see Daniel 12:2). This sleep is a metaphor which suggests that one day in the future those who have died will be awakened.

Why would Jesus or Paul use this word *sleep* instead of *death*? I believe that they used this word to soften the impact and trauma of death upon the bereaved loved ones.

To bring some clarification to this issue, it can help if we first know and understand the nature of man. Based on the psychological point of view, man is composed of two elements: body and soul. From the perspective of theologians, however, man is composed of three elements: spirit, soul and body. Both views are correct! This analysis, or anatomy, of the nature of man is only for the purpose of knowing and understanding the complex structure and the interrelationship of the elements of the human personality.

Man is an integrated being. He is basically a body and soul and either of these human elements is the integral and essential part of his existence. By this, I mean to say, the one can cannot survive without the other. When the word *body* is mentioned in the Bible, it is implied that the body has a soul. Conversely, when the word *soul* is mentioned, it is implicit with a body. The life of the body is the soul, and when the body dies, the soul dies as well.

The proponents of the doctrine that the soul is immortal misconstrue the meaning of Matthew 10:28, which states:

Do not fear those who kill the body but cannot kill the soul. But rather fear Him who is able to destroy both soul and body in hell.

This verse proves that the human soul is mortal and can be killed. When I asked one pastor who is a proponent of the immortal soul, the question, "What is killed in a body?" He could not answer. This is because what is killed in a body is the soul that gives it life. Therefore, when the body is killed, the soul is also killed, and the result is physical death.

The first part of this verse, which says, *"kill the body,"* is presumed to be a killing done by men. In the second part of the verse, Jesus said, *"but is not able to kill the soul."* What did He mean by this? This part of this verse has an eschatological dimension. At that point, the soul that cannot be killed has already attained immortality. Why? Because it has already been resurrected.

This explains why there are souls in Heaven in Revelation 6:9. They have been resurrected and have become immortal and so they are now in Heaven.

The Fall of man brought the tragic consequence of spiritual death to all mankind. So, death became a reality of life from then on, as Solomon said:

> *To everything there is a season,*
> *A time for every purpose under heaven:*
> *A time to be born,*
> *And a time to die.*   Ecclesiastes 3:1-2

Death is one appointment that no one can avoid.

The issue is whether or not the soul of man survives physical death. In other words: is the human soul immortal? Many pastors disagree with the definition of death I mentioned. They say that death is "separation." When I asked one of them, "What separates during death?" he answered, "The immaterial from the material." When I asked him again to elaborate o this, he did not answer. He

115

BLESSED ARE THE POOR

probably is referring to the separation of the soul from the body, meaning that the soul survives death.

What is worse: according to this group, after death the soul of man (assuming he is a committed Christian) immediately goes to Heaven. This doctrine is fallacious, and it entangles the subject with much error. There is no evidence in the Bible to support this contention. Instead, this doctrine is based on conjecture and speculation and is misleading. It has no legs to stand on when subjected to direct or collateral challenge.

God is immortal, and angels are immortal too, but not man. The Bible says clearly:

> *The soul who sins shall die.*   Ezekiel 18:4

So, when a man dies, his soul also dies. What soul are they talking about going to Heaven when it is already dead? As a rule, everyone will have to wait for the resurrection before he can attain immortality. This means that those Christians and Old Testament saints who have died already will not be conscious until their time of resurrection.

ETERNAL LIFE ELABORATED

And as Moses lifted up the serpent in the wilderness, even so must the Son of Man be lifted up, that whoever believes in Him should not perish but have eternal life. For God so loved the world that He gave His only begotten Son, that whoever believes in Him should not perish but have everlasting life. John 3:14-16

Everlasting, or eternal, life is imparted to man by God through faith in the Lord Jesus Christ. This is a God-kind of life, a life which is characteristic of Him.

The meaning of the phrase *eternal life* is "life without end" or "endless life." When we become born again, we receive eternal life. Based on the standard definition, however, true Christians should never die. This can be confusing. Hence the clarification: Christian belief and life are real and logical, not an illusion.

I believe that the promise of eternal life as a consequence of our relationship with our Lord Jesus Christ has two aspects. They are (1) the qualitative, and (2) the quantitative. What we received when we believed in Jesus is the qualitative aspect of eternal life. We have not yet realized the quantitative aspect;

it is for the future. The qualitative eternal life, however, is an *earnest* of the latter, meaning that it is the assurance of the future quantitative eternal life. This makes the promise of God to us binding. The challenge for Christians now is how to nurture and develop this qualitative eternal life so that we become like Christ.

This qualitative eternal life, however, does not guarantee that Christians will not die. The reason is that we are still mortal. The exception will be when Jesus returns.

This biblical perspective is consistent with the intent of God regarding the natural and spiritual status of man when He created him and as man was before the Fall. Although man was inbreathed by God with the breath of life (qualitative eternal life), this did not mean that man would not die. Man was still mortal. Otherwise, if man had been immortal, as many have believed and taught, why did God tell Adam that he would *"surely die"* if he ate from the forbidden tree (Genesis 2:7)? This breath of life produced the *"likeness"* (Genesis 1:26) of God" in man, so that man behaved like God. Sadly, however, man lost this divine imprint when he disobeyed God and fell.

Just because God is eternal (qualitatively and quantitatively) and He inbreathed man, many believe that man is also immortal. This is a terrible fallacy that entangles the subject with much error.

Jesus said:

I am the resurrection and the life. He who believes in Me, though he may die, he shall live. And whoever lives and believes in Me shall never die.   John 11:25-26

This is the quantitative eternal life. And when will it commence? At the Rapture (see 1 Thessalonians 4:13-18), when *"this mortal shall put on immortality"* (quantitative eternal life) (1 Corinthians 15:53).

Praise God! And glory to His name!

THE LIVING DEAD

But Jesus said to him, "Follow Me, and let the dead bury their own dead."   Matthew 8:22

Was Jesus talking about zombies here in this verse? Yes, He was — spiritual zombies, the living dead.

Paul talked a lot about such people in his epistles, saying, among other things, that they were *"dead in trespasses and sins"* (Ephesians 2:1, 5 and 13).

Nicodemus was one of the walking dead, and that's why Jesus told him he had to be born again (see John 3). The living dead are incomplete. They only have soul and body. To be a complete human being (spiritually alive), one needs to repent of his sins and accept Jesus Christ as his personal Lord and Savior. Then he becomes a completed person, being born again and with spirit, soul and body.

As Paul wrote:

Now may the God of peace Himself sanctify you completely; and may your whole spirit, soul, and body be preserved blameless at the coming of our Lord Jesus Christ.   1 Thessalonians 5:23

THE IMAGE AND LIKENESS OF GOD IN MAN

Then God said, "Let Us make man in Our image, according to Our likeness."   Genesis 1:26

Image and *likeness* ... Many believe that when man fell into sin, he lost one of these two divine imprints. The question is: which of the two was lost during the Fall?

I believe that what was lost was the likeness, and my evidence for this position is found in Genesis 9:6:

Whoever sheds man's blood,
By man his blood shall be shed;
For in the image of God
He made man.

Notice that only the phrase *image of God* is used here, not the phrase *likeness of God*. What does this tell us? Regardless of whether or not a person is a follower of Christ, he or she still bears the image of God. That's why we are forbidden by God to commit murder, because, in doing so, we strike the very image of God. (The exception, of course, is self-defense.)

What, then, is this image that we all have? Besides being a pastor, I am an amateur photographer, and what I know about an image is that it is a photo or a picture of something or someone. On this basis, I believe that you and I look like God, who has a body, with head, hands, feet, eyes, nose, ears and mouth. That is why Jesus, who was and is God, appeared on the earth looking like a man. In other words, this is the physical and the psychological feature of man which constitutes the human soul.

And what about *likeness*? This is the God-likeness of man which was lost in the Fall. Man was complete before the Fall; he was spirit, soul and body (see 1 Thessalonians 5:23).

The spirit of man is distinct from his soul. The spirit is the human element whereby he is conscious and in contact with God, the true God, Jesus Christ. The soul, which is the self-consciousness of man, has three areas: the mind, the emotions and the will.

The body is the world-consciousness of man: feel, touch and see. It was in the area of the spirit of man that this godlikeness resided, but when man sinned, his spirit died. Since then man has been spiritually dead even though he is physically alive. Paul explained that before we knew Christ, we were *"dead in [our] trespasses and sins"* (Ephesians 2:1).

The death contemplated as a consequence of sin was not physical but spiritual. Adam and Eve did not die physically at the moment they sinned against God, but they did die spiritually. And spiritual death is much worse than physical death. Spiritual death has eternal consequence, whereas physical death has only temporal consequence.

Have you ever heard someone say, "You look like your father, but you don't behave like him?" This is exactly the spiritual condition of man without Christ. So how do we recover this likeness of God? Jesus said:

You must be born again.   John 3:7

That which is born of the flesh is flesh, and that which is born of the Spirit is spirit.   John 3:6

The words that I speak to you are spirit, and they are life.
                                                    John 6:63

Man shall not live by bread alone, but by every word that proceeds from the mouth of God.   Matthew 4:4

I am the bread of life.   John 6:35

When the incarnate Word, who is Jesus Christ, is preached to people, the message of that Word is a spiritual seed which germinates in the soul of people so that they become born again. Thus, everyone who receives Jesus Christ into their lives has been granted the right to be a child of God.

The apostle Peter wrote:

For you have been born again, not of perishable seed, but of imperishable, through the living and enduring word of God.
                                              1 Peter 1:23, NIV

After the new birth, the lost divine imprint of the likeness of God in man is restored to a faithful, obedient and devoted Christian. Thus, the ideal Christian is like Christ. He thinks, speaks, behaves and lives like Jesus Christ, who always delighted to do the will of the father, and he does not continue in sin because God's seed remains in him (see 1 John 3:9).

Question: did some people in the Old Testament also recover the lost divine imprint of the likeness of God? I believe so. Retroactively, the Gospel was also preached to them, and those who believed by faith were justified (saved). One good example was Abraham. He was declared righteous because of his faith in God. When God spoke to him, Abraham was obedient to God, and this obedience was the effect of his spirit being restored to him through faith. That was the reason he responded so positively when God spoke to him.

Another example was David, who was dubbed as *"a man after his [God's] own heart"* (1 Samuel 13:14). David often had struggles and conflicts with his soul, but his spirit, which was restored, alive and strong in the Lord, prevailed over his soul.

For example, David said, *"Bless the Lord, O my soul"* (Psalm 103:1). In another instance, he said, "Why are you cast down, O my soul?" (Psalm 42:5). Who was talking to David's soul? It was his spirit!

Yes, like Abraham and David, we have our own weaknesses, struggles and conflicts, but we can overcome those — if we are strong in the Lord. And how can we become strong in the Lord? We must remain in Christ and He in us. We must continually and regularly nourish and feed ourselves with the pure spiritual milk of the Word of God so that we will grow up in our salvation. We must not compromise with sin and evil, but we must abhor those and cleave to that which is good.

> *I say then: Walk in the Spirit, and you shall not fulfill the lust of the flesh [sinful nature].*   Ephesians 5:16

In other words, we must not allow our soul to dominate our spirit, but our spirit must be dominant. There is an ongoing conflict between these two. So, if something inside you tells you to get up and go to church, to serve and worship God today because it is Sunday, that's good. It means that your spirit is alive.

If, on the other hand, something inside you tells you, "Sleep on. It's Sunday. Relax, there's no office or work today," that's not good. Either your spirit is dead or your soul is dominating.

What are the acts of the sinful nature? They are sexual immorality, impurity and debauchery, idolatry and witchcraft, hatred, discord, jealousy, fits of rage, envy, drunkenness, orgies and the like (see Galatians 5:19-21). In the Scriptures, this is followed by a serious warning:

> *I warn you, as I did before, that those who live like this will not inherit the kingdom of God.*   Galatians 5:21

And a serious admonition:

> *Since we live by the Spirit, let us keep in step with the Spirit.*
>   Galatians 5:25

THE ISSUE OF HUMAN MORTALITY

Then the LORD God took the man and put him in the garden of Eden to tend and keep it. And the LORD God commanded the man, saying, "Of every tree of the garden you may freely eat; but of the tree of the knowledge of good and evil you shall not eat, for in the day that you eat of it you shall surely die."   Genesis 2:15-17

When God commanded man (before his fall) not to eat of the tree of the knowledge of good and evil, He warned that in the day he ate of it, he would surely die (indicating mortality). The serpent rejected this admonition and assured the woman:

You will not surely die.   Genesis 3:4

Satan, in the form of a serpent, was arguing for man's immortality. So who was telling the truth and who was telling a lie? Of course God was telling the truth. He is Truth:

The LORD, the LORD God, merciful and gracious, longsuffering, and abounding in goodness and truth.   Exodus 34:6

And of course the serpent was telling the lie. He is a liar, and the Father of lies:

> *You are of your father the devil, and the desires of your father you want to do. He was a murderer from the beginning, and does not stand in the truth, because there is no truth in him. When he speaks a lie, he speaks from his own resources, for he is a liar and the father of it.* John 8:44

Those who subscribe to the belief that God created man mortal are of God, and those whose position is that man was created immortal are of the devil. Just like Eve, they are deceived.

Compact and Concise Christianity

And now abide faith, hope, love, these three; but the greatest of these is love.   1 Corinthians 13:13

Christianity is all about faith, hope and love. These three are intertwined and complement each other. Faith without love is nothing (see 1 Corinthians 13:2). Love always hopes, and faith is the evidence of the things we hope for (see Hebrews 11:1).

What is a Christian's faith? It is one segment of these three Christian doctrines that deal with the Christians' (followers of Christ's) trust or confidence in God through His Son Jesus Christ. Primarily, it has something to do with the salvation of man through the redemptive work of Christ on the cross of Calvary. We are saved by grace through faith in Jesus Christ (see Ephesians 2:8).

Faith is also the belief in the living God. Although we don't see Him, His power is evident through His creation. The reality of God is bolstered by the revelation of the incarnate Son of God and by the documentary evidence of the Holy Bible, which is the Word of God.

Faith encompasses and governs the entire life of a follower of Christ. The way he thinks or speaks and how he behaves or conducts himself in every relationship or situation is a practice of his faith.

This is not a blind faith, as some suggest, because a Christian is guided by the Word of God and by the Holy Spirit. He has knowledge and understanding of what the will of God is relative to his actions and decisions. It is through faith that we believe in God, and that's why we go to church and worship Him. It is through faith that we pray, because we believe that God answers prayer. It is through faith that we share with others the Good News of salvation in Jesus Christ. It is impossible to please God without faith (see Hebrews 11:6), and God rewards us when we believe.

But the most prominent among these three is love. Why? Because, according to Paul, it is love that validates all other Christian gifts — including faith. Without love, the other gifts would all amount to nothing.

God is love (see 1 John 4:8),and because every Christian is filled with God the Holy Spirit, he is also filled with God's love. This kind of love is more profound than the kind of love everybody is talking about today in our modern world, especially during holidays like Valentine's Day. That is the world's love, but this is the God-kind of love which is characterized by sacrifice. Jesus went to the cross because God loves every one of us.

The Christian's love acts in two directions. First, it is toward God (vertically) and then toward his fellow being (horizontally). This is consistent with what Jesus said when He summarized the Ten Commandments into two:

"You shall love the Lord your God with all your heart, with all your soul, and with all your mind." This is the first and great

commandment. And the second is like it: "You shall love your
neighbor as yourself."   Matthew 22:37-39

The image that is formed from the two directions of a Christian's love forms a cross. I believe this is what Jesus meant when He said:

If anyone desires to come after Me, let him deny himself, and take
up his cross, and follow Me.   Matthew 16:24

The Christian's love of God forms his lifetime devotion and dedication, but as followers of Christ, Christians also love one another. In fact, Christians are the most loving, caring, generous, patient and helpful people in the world. The most loving husbands, wives, children and families are Christians. Christians even love their enemies. How do they show this? By doing good to them.

A Christian's hope is something that is expected to happen in the future. We always look forward to something good and positive. Our hope is based on the promises of God in the Bible. There is a temporal hope, and there is an ultimate (eternal) hope. Despite the many trials and hardships of life, Christians are the most hopeful people in the world. They are blessed with perseverance in education, hard work, diligence, honesty, savings and blessings — all through Divine Providence. Christians are always hopeful of a better life, both here in this world and also in the world to come. They live in sufficiency and contentment with peace and joy in the Lord.

Of course, the ultimate Christian hope is otherwise known as *"the Blessed Hope"*:

For the grace of God that brings salvation has appeared to all men, teaching us that, denying ungodliness and worldly lusts, we should live soberly, righteously, and godly in the present age, looking for THE BLESSED HOPE and glorious appearing of our great God and Savior Jesus Christ, who gave Himself for us, that He might redeem us from every lawless deed and purify for Himself His own special people, zealous for good works. Speak these things. Titus 2:11-15, Emphasis Mine

Christ's return will be one of the greatest events in history. It will be then that those who have died in Christ will be resurrected, and those who are alive will be changed and given glorified bodies. Then, together, we will all meet the Lord in the air and go to be with Him in Heaven:

For this we say to you by the word of the Lord, that we who are alive and remain until the coming of the Lord will by no means precede those who are asleep. For the Lord Himself will descend from heaven with a shout, with the voice of an archangel, and with the trumpet of God. And the dead in Christ will rise first. Then we who are alive and remain shall be caught up together with them in the clouds to meet the Lord in the air. And thus we shall always be with the Lord. Therefore comfort one another with these words. 1 Thessalonians 4:15-18

This will be the moment John spoke of in his Revelation:

And God will wipe away every tear from their eyes; there shall be no more death, nor sorrow, nor crying. There shall be no more pain, for the former things have passed away. Revelation 21:4

Jesus is coming again — and soon! Are you ready to meet Him? Don't be left behind. If you are not ready yet, then today is your day of salvation. Don't wait for tomorrow, when it may be too late. Call upon the Lord now. Ask His forgiveness for your sins, and receive Him as your Lord and Savior, and you will be saved.

Once you have done that, choose to live for Him the rest of your life, for the best is yet to come!

CONSTANTLY CONTENTED CHRISTIANS

Let your conduct be without covetousness; be content with such things as you have. For He Himself has said, "I will never leave you nor forsake you." Hebrews 13:5

One of the moral imperatives for Christians has always been contentment. The writer to the Hebrews advised: *"Be content with such things as you have."* Why? Because God has said that He will never leave us or forsake us.

When John the Baptist preached to the people of his day about God's judgment coming unless they showed fruits of repentance, the people responded by asking him:

What shall we do then? Luke 3:10

When soldiers who were present asked him that question, he responded:

Do not intimidate anyone or accuse falsely, and be content with your wages. Luke 3:14

The exhortation in Hebrews 13 to Christians to be content is also connected to the issue of money. Paul added to this by stating:

> *And having food and clothing, with these we shall be content. But those who desire to be rich fall into temptation and a snare, and into many foolish and harmful lusts which drown men in destruction and perdition. For the love of money is a root of all kinds of evil, for which some have strayed from the faith in their greediness, and pierced themselves through with many sorrows.*
> 1 Timothy 6:8-10

This was exactly what happened to Judas, one of the original disciples of our Lord Jesus Christ. Judas loved money, so he betrayed, or sold, Jesus for thirty pieces of silver. In so doing, he plunged himself into perdition.

What is the opposite of contentment? It is covetousness. It is greed. It is the insatiable desire for one to acquire money and things which are not our own, even to the prejudice of other people. The reality of this avarice fills not only the headlines of our media today, but the whole of modern society. Corruption has become the culture of the day. The morality of so many people is all about money, lots of it.

What is disgusting, disgraceful and revolting is that when those who are supposed to be respected lawmakers and law-enforcers are the ones who become lawbreakers themselves. For example, here in our country legislators were indicted for plundering government funds in the amount of more than ₱50 million and policemen had to be apprehended because they were suspected of crimes of robbery (hulidap), extortion, murder and kidnapping for ransom. Too often, our government systems are filled with corruption, and there is only one reason for all of this systematic hooliganism — the love of money.

Followers of Christ are precluded from engaging in or being involved in any form of covetousness. The Bible states emphatically: *"Thou shalt not covet"* (Exodus 20:17, KJV). Why? Because if you covet, you will also cheat, lie and steal.

The tragic story of Achan in the book of Joshua is a stern warning, not only to Christians, but also to all people everywhere, of the evil consequences of covetousness. He confessed:

When I saw among the spoils a beautiful Babylonian garment, two hundred shekels of silver, and a wedge of gold weighing fifty shekels, I coveted them and took them. And there they are, hidden in the earth in the midst of my tent, with the silver under it.
                                                                    Joshua 7:21

It was a fatal mistake for Achan, for it not only cost him his life, it cost the lives of his children as well. His sin of covetousness also brought defeat to Israel at the hand of her enemies that day.

Christians, whether they are poor or rich, are the most contented people in the world. This means they are satisfied with whatever they have, in terms of money or the things they possess. They do not cheat, lie or steal other people's money or things. They are the most honest and trustworthy people on earth. Whereas covetous people only think of what or how they can get something from other people, Christians are always thinking of what or how they can give something to others, especially to the poor and needy. Christians are generous and kind people.

In the first part of the book I mentioned the Ek family of Sweden who have given so much to so many. That's what true Christians are like.

Why are Christians so contented? The answer goes back to our original text. It is because God has said that He will never leave us or forsake us. David knew it and sang:

> The LORD is my shepherd;
> I shall not want.   Psalm 23:1

One of the names of God is Jehovah Jireh (God who provides). That's why Christians don't worry about what they are going to eat or drink or what they will wear because our heavenly Father knows our needs (see Matthew 6:25). As noted in an earlier teaching, God will meet all your needs according to His glorious riches in Christ Jesus (see Philippians 4:19). Jesus said it this way:

> But seek first the kingdom of God and His righteousness, and all these things shall be added to you.   Matthew 6:33

As Paul wrote to Timothy:

> Godliness with contentment is great gain.   1 Timothy 6:6

FROM THE PRISON TO THE PALACE

And the LORD was with Joseph, and he was a prosperous man; and he was in the house of his master the Egyptian. And his master saw that the LORD was with him, and that the LORD made all that he did to prosper in his hand. And Joseph found grace in his sight, and he served him: and he made him overseer over his house, and all that he had he put into his hand.   Genesis 39:2-4

The man called Joseph in the book of Genesis is one of the most sensational and inspiring of biblical characters. In Chapter 41, Joseph was summoned by Pharaoh, the king of Egypt, to his palace. This moment was crucial because it would change the situation of Joseph and his family for the better. This change would also affect the survival of the entire Jewish nation.

The reason Joseph was summoned by Pharaoh to the palace was because he wanted him to interpret one of his dreams. But, at the moment, Joseph was in prison. He had been falsely accused by the wife of Potiphar, captain of the king's guard, of attempted rape.

Potiphar had bought Joseph as a slave. Joseph's jealous brothers had sold him to some Ishmaelites who were passing through Canaan, and they sold him to Potiphar in Egypt. But as the text indicates, the Lord was with Joseph in Potiphar's house, and God blessed Potiphar because of Joseph. Potiphar's wife, however, was jealous of Joseph, so she tried to seduce him and then falsely accused him when he refused her.

While Joseph was in prison, God gave him favor in the sight of the prison warden, so that he was in charge of the whole prison. There he met two of Pharaoh's servants.

These men had both displeased the king and had been imprisoned in the very same prison with Joseph. One night they both had a dream and could not interpret it. Joseph, however, was able to interpret their dreams. Just as he foretold in his interpretation, within three days, the king's baker was executed, and the king's butler was restored to his position.

The butler had agreed to remember Joseph when he was restored to his job, but he forgot. Then, after two more years had gone by, Pharaoh dreamed a dream, and it was repeated twice. It was such a bizarre dream that he was deeply troubled by it. He called for the wise men in his palace to help interpret the dream, but none of them were able to do so. The butler, who had been with Joseph in prison, now remembered him and told Pharaoh about his ability to interpret dreams. And that was how Joseph happened to be summoned to the palace.

When the matter was placed before Joseph, he answered Pharaoh wisely:

It is not in me: God shall give Pharaoh an answer of peace.
Genesis 41:16

And it happened just as Joseph had said. God showed him that there would be seven years of plenty in the land followed by seven years of famine. His recommendation to the Pharaoh was to look for a man who could oversee the gathering of twenty percent of all the harvests throughout Egypt during the seven good years in preparation for the coming famine. The result was that Joseph himself was chosen by Pharaoh to be that man, and he was soon appointed ruler over all Egypt, except in matters of the throne.

Although the circumstances and situations in the life of Joseph changed, one thing was constant: whether he was in Potiphar's house or in the prison, the Lord was with him, and the Lord made him to prosper. As followers of Christ, we can emulate Joseph's trust in God in any and all adverse circumstances and situations in life, knowing full well what He has promised:

Never will I leave you; never will I forsake you.
Hebrews 13:5, NIV

And we know that in all things God works for the good of those who love him, who have been called according to his purpose.
Romans 8:28, NIV

Praise the Lord! Hallelujah!

PRAYERS THAT PREVAIL

In this manner, therefore, pray:

Our Father in heaven,
Hallowed be Your name.
Your kingdom come.
Your will be done
On earth as it is in heaven.
Give us this day our daily bread.
And forgive us our debts,
As we forgive our debtors.
And do not lead us into temptation,
But deliver us from the evil one.
For Yours is the kingdom and the power and the glory forever.
Amen!   Matthew 6:9-13

As Christians, we believe in prayer. This is one of our essential Christian practices. We pray because our God is alive, and He hears and answers our prayers. But why is it that so many of our prayers seem to be ineffective and go unanswered. Let us examine some possible reasons.

One of the reasons our payers may be ineffective and un-answered is because they are lacking in form and substance. Our Lord Jesus Christ taught us how to pray, and this is how a Christian should pray. This prayer is known to many as "The Lord's Prayer," but I prefer to call it "The Christians' Prayer." It is a pattern, or a model, for our prayers.

First of all, we should address God as our Father when we pray. Addressing God as Father in prayers has many far-reaching implications or benefits for us. We must acknowledge Him as Sovereign and as our Creator, etc. It is only then that we should mention our various needs. Some of them are physical, others are financial or material, and there are prayer needs which re-quire supernatural intervention. Finally, all these things must be concluded by asking in the name of Jesus.

Jesus Himself said:

Whatever you ask in My name, that I will do, that the Father may be glorified in the Son. John 14:13

In that day you will ask in My name. John 16:26

We must learn how to properly pray. Just as Jesus taught His disciples to pray, pastors are tasked with teaching their members to pray. We cannot just assume that when a person is already saved they will automatically know how to pray. Most prayers that I hear are copy-cat prayers, improper prayers and prayers full of redundancy and nonsense. Sometimes we wish that the person praying would stop or that they had never prayed at all.

Some people make prayer an art. Their prayers are dotted with much repetition and flowery language that means very little. The truth is that we are precluded by the Lord from using this kind of language in prayer. Jesus taught:

> *And when you pray, you shall not be like the hypocrites. For they love to pray standing in the synagogues and on the corners of the streets, that they may be seen by men.* Matthew 6:5

> *And when you pray, do not use vain repetitions as the heathen do. For they think that they will be heard for their many words.*
> Matthew 6:7

Some Christians even shout when they pray. God is not deaf, so you don't need to shout at Him. Speak politely to God.

Others pray without ever opening their mouths or uttering words. This is not prayer; it is meditation. People do this especially when they pray before eating in a restaurant. Are they embarrassed to pray? Or do they simply not know how to pray?

If we want our prayers to be more powerful and more effective, besides the aforementioned proper form and substance, try coupling prayer with fasting. When the disciples of our Lord asked Him why they were unsuccessful in casting out demons, His answer was:

> *This kind can come out by nothing but prayer and fasting.*
> Mark 9:9

Try it. You'll be surprised.

RICH MAN, POOR MAN
(A REVERSAL OF FORTUNES)

Then Jesus said to His disciples, "Assuredly, I say to you that it is hard for a rich man to enter the kingdom of heaven. And again I say to you, it is easier for a camel to go through the eye of a needle than for a rich man to enter the kingdom of God."

Matthew 19:23-24

Why did Jesus pronounce these strong words against the rich? This was His response concerning the rich young man who came to Him asking how he could obtain eternal life. The man was told by Jesus to sell his possessions and give the proceeds to the poor and follow Him, so that he would have treasures in Heaven. But the man was unhappy when he heard this, and he turned away sorrowful. The reason? Because he had great possessions.

What happened to that rich man? He went back to his business, and he had bumper harvests on his farms. He had so much produce that he had to tear down his barns and build larger ones in order to store all of his grain and goods. Then he said to his soul, "Soul, you have plenty of goods laid up for many years. Relax, eat and have a good time" (see Luke 12:16-21).

The rich man was enjoying his success, buying the best clothes and having sumptuous meals every day, but there was also a poor man, and this poor man came to the rich man's house to beg:

But there was a certain beggar named Lazarus, full of sores, who was laid at his gate, desiring to be fed with the crumbs which fell from the rich man's table. Moreover the dogs came and licked his sores.   Luke 16:20

Subsequently, Lazarus died and was carried by the angels into Abraham's bosom. The rich man also died:

The rich man also died and was buried, and his soul went to the place of the dead. There, in torment, he saw Abraham in the far distance with Lazarus at his side. The rich man shouted, "Father Abraham, have some pity! Send Lazarus over here to dip the tip of his finger in water and cool my tongue. I am in anguish in these flames."
But Abraham said to him, "Son, remember that during your lifetime you had everything you wanted, and Lazarus had nothing. So now he is here being comforted, and you are in anguish."
                                          Luke 16:22-25, NLT

What a reversal of fortunes!
As Jesus said:

For what will it profit a man if he gains the whole world, and loses his own soul?   Mark 8:36

When Jesus said that it would be difficult for a rich man to enter into the Kingdom of Heaven, the disciples were very surprised and asked Him:

Rich Man, Poor Man

Who then can be saved?   Matthew 19:25

His answer was this:

With men this is impossible; but with God all things are possible.   *Matthew 19:26*

We all need God to save us. That's why He sent His Son that whoever believes in Him might have eternal life. What must you do? Repent of your sins now and receive Jesus as your personal Lord and Savior. Find a Bible-believing church. Serve God and fellowship with the family of God. Follow Jesus the rest of your life, and you will be saved.

If you are a Christian, do not desire to be rich. Why? Because in order to achieve your desire, you will be tempted to lie, to cheat, to steal and to defraud other people, putting your soul at risk. If a Christian is diligent, industrious and smart, and God blesses him so that he becomes rich, then that is all right.

If you are a rich Christian, do not be proud or trust in your riches, but in God who is the Source of all riches. Be rich in doing charitable works, thereby laying up for yourself treasures in Heaven. These kinds of treasures have eternal values.

TEACHING 14

SIGNS, SPECTACLES AND SYMBOLS

But I will make Pharaoh's heart stubborn so I can multiply my miraculous signs and wonders in the land of Egypt.

Exodus 7:3, NLT

The reluctant and hesitant Moses finally decided to return to Egypt and deliver the Israelites out of Egyptian bondage. Prior to this decision, he had made excuses as to why he could not go back there. Two of his excuses were: (1) They will not believe me or listen to me, and (2) I have a speech impediment. So, what convinced Moses and changed his mind? The Lord demonstrated to him miraculous signs in response to his excuses.

For the first sign, the Lord told Moses to throw his staff on the ground. When he did this, it turned into a snake, and he ran from it. Then the Lord told him to take the snake by the tail, and when he did this, it turned into a staff again.

For the second sign, the Lord told Moses to put his hand under his cloak, and when he took his hand out, it had become leprous. When he put his hand back in and then took it out again, it was restored. Then the Lord said to him:

And it shall be, if they do not believe even these two signs, or listen to your voice, that you shall take water from the river and pour it on the dry land. The water which you take from the river will become blood on the dry land. Exodus 4:9

Convinced and confident with these signs, Moses went back to Egypt. He would first have to persuade the Israelites and then persuade Pharaoh, King of Egypt, regarding God's plan of deliverance for His people.

Upon his arrival, Moses was met by his brother Aaron, and they gathered together all the elders of Israel. Aaron relayed to them everything the Lord had said to Moses. He also performed the signs before them, and they believed, bowed down and worshipped.

But when Moses and Aaron went to Pharaoh and told him that God had said, *"Let My people go,"* he refused and, instead, made the labor of the Israelites harsher, imposing even heavier burdens on them. Because of these aggravating circumstances, the Israelites no longer wanted to listen to Moses. They were discouraged by reason of the cruel bondage exacted by Pharaoh.

Moses and Aaron returned to Pharaoh, and they were asked to perform a miracle. Aaron threw his staff in front of Pharaoh, and it became a snake. This was imitated by Pharaoh's magicians, but their snakes were swallowed up by Aaron's snake. Still, the result was disappointing:

And Pharaoh's heart grew hard, and he did not heed them, as the LORD *had said.* Exodus 7:13

Now God had to demonstrate His spectacle, otherwise known as the Ten Plagues of Egypt. They were the plagues of blood, frogs, gnats, flies, diseased livestock, boils, hail, locusts, darkness and, finally, the plague on the firstborn. In the beginning of these plagues, Pharaoh's magicians tried to imitate them, but soon they gave up and declared: *"This is the finger of God"* (Exodus 8:19).

It is interesting to note that during these calamities, the Lord made a distinction between the Egyptians and the Israelites. While there was tremendous devastation among all of the Egyptians, no one among the Israelites suffered. This was a sign in itself.

Crucial and decisive among these plagues was the death of the firstborn, also known as the Passover. This was the last of the plagues, and it killed all the firstborn of the Egyptians, including the firstborn of Pharaoh, together with their animals.

The passing of the death angel did not adversely affect the Israelites. The Lord had instructed Moses and Aaron to prepare special lambs, about a year old and without defect, for that particular evening. Each Israelite household must take one of those lambs and kill it at twilight. They were to take some blood from their lamb and put it on the sides and tops of the door frames of the houses, where they would eat the lamb roasted. This blood was to be a sign, and when the Lord saw the blood, no destructive plague would touch His people.

The Lord proceeded to strike down all the firstborn in Egypt that night at the stroke of midnight, including the firstborn of Pharaoh, and so there was death in every Egyptian home that night. Finally, it was too much for Pharaoh to bear, and he released the Israelites and gave them their freedom. This was a day that Israel would commemorate for generations to come — a lasting ordinance, a festival unto the Lord.

What have these Old Testament narratives got to do with us contemporary Christians? Is there any relevance or significance to our Christian faith? What about those signs, the spectacle and the symbols? Are these important or helpful? The answer is affirmative. As followers of Christ, we must understand that the Old and New Testaments are intertwined. Whereas, to the early Christians, the Old Testament was sacred Scripture, to us contemporary Christians, we recognize both the Old and New Testaments as our sacred Scriptures.

Now, are signs or miracles still relevant or significant today? Simply put, does God do miracles or heal people today through His servants? Many people, including many Christians, say that the days of miracles are over, but I still believe in miracles because our God is a God of miracles.

Among the fastest-growing Christian churches during this and the past century have been the various Pentecostal groups. We can observe their phenomenal evangelistic success in North and South America and Europe, but also in Asia and Africa. The reason, I believe, for their dramatic success is their evangelistic strategy. Their Gospel persuasion is coupled with signs and wonders. After preaching the Gospel and challenging people to commit their lives to Christ, they always conclude with prayer for the sick and for miracles. If people do not yet believe their message, then the signs of healing and miracles will validate the veracity of their words.

This was the same predicament Moses faced. He was afraid that his own people as well as Pharaoh would not believe him or listen to him. God used the same signs that had convinced Moses to take on the task to convince the Israelites and Pharaoh. Jesus said:

If I do not do the works of My Father, do not believe Me; but if I do, though you do not believe Me, believe the works, that you may know and believe that the Father is in Me, and I in Him.

John 10:37-38

149

Of course, if there is a genuine miracle, then there is also a fake one, just as there are true prophets and false prophets. The false always wants to copy the true. Fakes are everywhere, even today.

How about symbols? The Bible is filled with many symbols. Some of them are difficult to interpret. Sometimes those symbols are also known as "shadows." For instance, the Passover lamb was a symbol, or shadow, of Jesus Christ, the Lamb of God who takes away the sins of the world. His suffering, His death on the cross and the shedding of His blood were acts of redemption. Peter wrote:

> *You were not redeemed with corruptible things, like silver or gold, from your aimless conduct received by tradition from your fathers, but with the precious blood of Christ, as of a lamb without blemish and without spot.* 1 Peter 1:18-19

Just as the firstborn of the Israelites were spared from death that Passover night because they appropriated the blood of a sacrificial lamb on their door frames, so also everyone who believes in Jesus Christ will not perish but will have eternal life.

We Christians remember the redemptive sacrifice of our Lord Jesus Christ in the Communion, one of our traditional Christian worship rituals. The bread which is broken and taken by members symbolizes the body of Christ, and the wine symbolizes His blood. Thus, every Christian partakes of Christ's sacrifice in Communion.

The Ideal Christian Mind

Let this mind be in you which was also in Christ Jesus.

Philippians 2:5

One of the important areas of a Christian's life which needs change — radical change — is his mind. As a matter of fact, repentance must take place in that person's mind. One must be convinced in his mind of the truth of the Gospel of Jesus Christ and that believing and receiving Him as personal Lord and Savior is the only way to salvation.

How important is this mind change? It is very important because it will affect and determine the spiritual and secular dimensions of the person, as well as his eternal perspective on life. It is from a person's mind that an attitude is formed, depending on the information received. Then, from the person's attitude emanates his behaviors. Compared with the computer, the mind is the central processing unit of the person.

The mind is one element of the human soul, the others being the emotions and the will. The mind is the seat of our human intellect and reason. It is where our thinking processes come from. In the Bible, however, a person's mind is referred to as his "heart." For example: the book of Proverbs says, *"As [a man] thinks in his heart, so is he"* (Proverbs 23:7). Jesus said:

> *For from within, out of the heart of men, proceed evil thoughts, adulteries, fornications, murders, thefts, covetousness, wicked-ness, deceit, lewdness, an evil eye, blasphemy, pride, foolishness. All these evil things come from within and defile a man.*
>
> Mark 7:21-23

To the Jewish understanding, these two terms — the mind and the heart — were to be used interchangeably. They are similar, forming the very core of a person's human personality, and that is very interesting.

Paul wrote:

> *Therefore, if anyone is in Christ, he is a new creation; old things have passed away; behold, all things have become new.*
>
> 2 Corinthians 5:17

There is a transition here, a change, from the old to the new. What are the things that have changed? Surely, this person is the same person, with the same face and in a similar social or economic status. But what has changed is his mind. Before he received Jesus Christ into his life, his mind was reprobate, perverted, corrupt, carnal, blinded to spiritual things and without knowledge and understanding. Now that he is in Christ Jesus, it is totally different. This person has a changed mind, the mind of Christ!

Two important questions are: (1) How does a Christian think like Christ? and (2) What are the things that he should think? First of all, the Christian, following the example of Jesus Christ, must always think about humility and obedience. Although Jesus was

God, He humbled Himself and became a servant and He was obedient to the will of the Father, even to death on the cross (see Philippians 2:8). Secondly, the Christian should think about things which are true, noble and right:

Finally, brethren, whatever things are true, whatever things are noble, whatever things are just, whatever things are pure, whatever things are lovely, whatever things are of good report, if there is any virtue and if there is anything praiseworthy — meditate on these things. Philippians 4:8

Therefore, as God's chosen people, holy and dearly loved, clothe yourselves with compassion, kindness, humility, gentleness and patience. Colossians 3:12, NIV

The opposite of these were our former thoughts, which were filled with sexual immorality, impurity, lust, evil desires and greed, which are all another form of idolatry. A Christian must also discard all thoughts of anger, rage, malice, slander, filthy language and lies.

A Christian should think about Heaven. Too many only think of it when they are dying. Paul taught that, as Christians:

Since, then, you have been raised with Christ, set your hearts on things above, where Christ is, seated at the right hand of God. Colossians 3:1, NIV

Jesus is preparing a place for us in Heaven, and He will come again and take us to be with Him. So, let us remember that, as Christians, our citizenship is in Heaven, and this world is not our home. We are just passing through here. One day we are going Home. That is why Jesus said:

> *Do not lay up for yourselves treasures on earth, where moth and rust destroy and where thieves break in and steal; but lay up for yourselves treasures in heaven, where neither moth nor rust destroys and where thieves do not break in and steal. For where your treasure is, there your heart will be also.*
>
> Matthew 6:19-21

Why are we not to lay up treasures here? Because the things in this world are temporal, while heavenly things are eternal. There will be no more curse or sickness there, for God will wipe away the tears from our eyes, and there will be no more death, only eternal bliss in the beauty of Paradise and the splendor of the Holy City, New Jerusalem, forever. Oh, it's wonderful to think about Heaven!

Earlier I mentioned about the three elements of the human soul, namely: the mind, the emotions and the will. In reality, and oftentimes, there are contentions and tensions between the mind and the emotions. Whichever prevails becomes the will of that person, which boils down to his decision on the particular issue or issues he is currently confronted with. When we allow our emotions to overrule our reason (mind), there are always problems, big problems, as a consequence. However, if we allow our reason to dominate, we become callous and insensitive, especially when people are involved. There must be a balance between these two if we are to arrive at favorable and reasonable decisions in life. As a rule, the emotions must be subservient to reason (the mind) so that we can avoid bigger problems.

There is another player in this decision dilemma of man, which is more confined to Christians. This concerns the will of God. After the struggle between the emotions and our reason (the mind), which results in the will of man, now comes the struggle between the will of man and the will of God. As Christians, we want to always do the will of God relative to whatever decision or actions we wish to takes. But how can we know and understand that what we decide to do is the will of God? It's a good question.

There is the general will of God, and there is the particular will of God. The general will of God is revealed in the Bible relative to our life's issues. The particular will of God is not written in the Bible, but there are similar principles that can be applied. One needs to be patient and wait, consult and seek advice from pastors or elders, and utter lots of prayers if he or she wants to know and walk in the particular will of God.

Paul wrote:

I beseech you therefore, brethren, by the mercies of God, that you present your bodies a living sacrifice, holy, acceptable to God, which is your reasonable service. And do not be conformed to this world, but be transformed by the renewing of your mind, that you may prove what is that good and acceptable and perfect will of God.   Romans 12:1-2

LOVE OR LUST?

Do not love the world or anything in the world. If anyone loves the world, love for the Father is not in them. For everything in the world — the lust of the flesh, the lust of the eyes, and the pride of life — comes not from the Father but from the world.

1 John 2:15-16

One of the hallmarks of Christianity is having love toward others. The God whom we Christians worship and serve is a God of love. Followers of Christ are mandated to love God with all their heart, their mind, their soul, their strength and also to love their neighbors as themselves. It is love that validates all the grace of gifts in the Church. Without love, the exercise of gifts mean nothing. That is how important love is to the Christian faith.

Not all love, however, is acceptable to God. There is a wrong kind of love that Christians are precluded from being involved with. This is the *"love of the world."* The word *world* in this passage does not refer to the physical world that God created. And neither does it refer to the world of mankind, because God loves both of these worlds. For example, the Bible shows that we are

156

in the world [the physical world and mankind], but we are not *of* this world [the worldly system]. Jesus said:

> *They are not of the world, just as I am not of the world.*
>
> John 17:16

This has reference to systems like "the world of entertainment," the "world of sports," the "world of business," etc. It refers to the trends and cultures of the people of this world who are opposed to God and are influenced and inspired by the devil, who is the god of this world. Such systems or lifestyles are contrary to God and His order. These are characterized by lust and wickedness.

The 2014 case of the murder of the Filipino race-car driver, Ferdinand "Enzo" Pastor is relevant to this divine injunction. The "love" of the wife's alleged lover was a wrong kind of love. She was a married woman, so he had no right to love her. When a man loves a woman who is married, that love is driven by lust — the lust of the flesh and the lust of the eyes. It is immoral, illicit and illegal. In this case, it was also deadly, because the result was that her husband was murdered. This is one situation where divorce (although I personally don't like it) might have been a more acceptable option. It might have been a lesser evil or, as some say, "a necessary evil." Instead of killing a mate, we should live and let live. Let the guilty party stand before the law and before God.

What happened to Enzo is nothing new. There was a similar case of a dangerous love triangle a long time ago in the Bible involving King David, a woman named Bathsheba and her husband Uriah. David lusted after Bathsheba, even after he knew that she was a married woman. In order to legitimize his relationship with her, he devised a sinister plot to murder Uriah. Conveniently, Uriah was killed in the heat of battle against Israel's enemies.

But this thing that David had done displeased the Lord. David's love for the woman trumped his love for God, and through the prophet Nathan, God sternly rebuked David because of his sin. Although David repented of his sin and regretted his actions, the price he paid in pain, agony and untold misery were not worth the pleasure of his misadventure with Bathsheba. His deep remorse for his sin is reflected in Psalm 51, for he was saved by the grace and mercy of God, but four of David's children perished, some of them in a scandalous manner, all as a consequences of his sinful lust.

How can anyone determine the difference between love and lust? When any love for a woman or man has a sign over it which says FORBIDDEN (in Tagalog, BAWAL) and you get involved anyway, that is lust.

But how do we know that it is forbidden? It is forbidden when the object of your love, whether a man or a woman, is married. This is a divine injunction, and it also applies to things like money, for example:

> *For the love of money is a root of all kinds of evil, for which some have strayed from the faith in their greediness, and pierced themselves through with many sorrows.*　　　1 Timothy 6:10

How can anyone avoid lust? The Bible says:

> *Walk in the Spirit, and you shall not fulfill the lust of the flesh.*
> Galatians 5:16

This is akin to the command to *"walk by faith and not by sight"* (2 Corinthians 5:7). This means that Christians are motivated by the Word of God. His Word is His Spirit. Jesus said:

LOVE OR LUST?

It is the Spirit who gives life; the flesh profits nothing. The words that I speak to you are spirit, and they are life. John 6:63

Christians must not be motivated by what they see, feel, think or want. Love or lust? You have been warned! Don't be stupid! Be wise and stay away from trouble — big trouble!

A PATTERN FOR PRAYER

So He said to them, "When you pray, say:

'Our Father in heaven,
Hallowed be Your name.
Your kingdom come.
Your will be done
On earth as it is in heaven.
Give us day by day our daily bread.
And forgive us our sins,
For we also forgive everyone who is indebted to us.
And do not lead us into temptation,
But deliver us from the evil one.' " Luke 11:2-4

After Jesus had finished praying one day, one of His disciples asked Him, *"Lord, teach us to pray, as John also taught his disciples"* (verse 1). In response, Jesus first warned the disciples against the futility of copy-cat prayers, which are motivated by hypocrisy and filled with meaningless redundancy. Then He said to them, *"When you pray, say ..."* and He taught them what is commonly called "The

Lord's Prayer." I prefer to call it "The Christians Prayer" because it is Christians who are to use it.

However, we are not to pray this prayer verbatim. It is not a prayer to be memorized and repeated over and over. Rather it is a model for prayer. In modern terms, this is a *template* for prayer.

When Jesus said, *"When you pray, say ... ,"* He meant, "Pray like this." This prayer pattern is implicit with form and substance, which, when carefully observed, will make our Christian prayers easier and meaningful. The form is the structure, the skeleton or the framework. Let's simplify this form into Step 1, Step 2 and Step 3.

Step 1 is the beginning of the Christian prayer.

Our Father in heaven: According to Jesus, we must address our prayers to our heavenly Father. It is unfortunate that many Christians do not follow this. Addressing God as *"heavenly Father"* in our prayers has significant implications. God is our Father by means of Creation, and He is our Father through redemption in Jesus Christ.

Your kingdom come, Your will be done on earth as it is in heaven: We must acknowledge God's sovereignty and power, including His will for our individual lives. This will require knowledge and understanding of Him and also of His Word.

Step 2 is focused on our human needs.

Give us day by day our daily bread: What do we need? What are our basic requirements? Basically, we need food, clothing, shelter, money and good health.

And forgive us our sins, for we also forgive everyone who is indebted to us: We need love and forgiveness. We also need peace and freedom from fear. Most of all, we need God. In other words, our needs are physical, emotional and spiritual. This is consistent with our complete human nature, which is composed of body, soul and spirit. Other people have needs too, so we must pray for them as well.

Prayer is not always asking things from God, but we pray to also give thanks to Him for all His blessings. As far as human need is concerned, our prayers may vary. It could be a petition, an intercession or a prayer of gratitude (thanksgiving).

Step 3 is the conclusion of this prayer.

Christian prayer must be concluded by asking all things in the name of Jesus.

So, what should be the substance of our prayer? It should not be only the contents of Step 2. The words expressed in prayer should include all three steps.

Remember, prayer is your most important conversation. Why? Because you are talking with God Almighty, the King of Kings and the Lord of Lords Himself. So, be careful with your words. The words of your prayer are expressions of what's in your heart. Therefore, be discreet and discerning of your every utterance in prayer. Sometimes you may even want to rehearse your prayers before saying them to be sure they are biblical.

THE PRINCE WHO CHOSE TO BE A SLAVE

By faith Moses, when he became of age, refused to be called the son of Pharaoh's daughter, choosing rather to suffer affliction with the people of God than to enjoy the passing pleasures of sin, esteeming the reproach of Christ greater riches than the treasures in Egypt; for he looked to the reward.   Hebrews 11:24-26

Moses is an interesting, intriguing and exciting Bible character. He was an extraordinary person. The circumstances surrounding his life were filled with sensational drama. His decisions and actions were critical to bringing about, not only a turning point in his own life, but also in the whole nation of Israel. The entire nation was delivered from slavery in Egypt by the mighty hand of God revealed through Moses.

God had blessed the Israelites during their sojourn in Egypt, beginning with the time of Joseph, and they had greatly increased in number. But when there arose another Pharaoh who did not know Joseph, he became hostile to and suspicious of them. This Pharaoh, or king, of Egypt, devised a scheme to stop the rapid increase of the Israelite population — the killing of all their male babies. This was achieved by throwing them into the Nile River. It was during these dark and dangerous times that Moses was born.

Moses' mother was courageous and did not fear the king's edict. She hid her son from those who were taking the babies. When she could no longer hide him, she made a basket of papyrus straw and placed her son in it. Then she placed the basket among the reeds along the banks of the Nile, leaving Miriam, Moses' older sister to watch it.

It just so happened that Pharaoh's daughter had gone to the river to bathe that day, and she saw the basket. Curious, she asked for it to be brought to her. When the basket was opened, she saw the baby and immediately knew, "This is one of the Hebrew babies."

About that time Miriam appeared and approached Pharaoh's daughter and asked, "Shall I get one of the Hebrew women to nurse the baby for you?"

"Yes, go," the princess answered, and the girl went and got her own mother.

When Moses' mother had arrived, Pharaoh's daughter said to her, "Take this baby and nurse him for me, and I will pay you." In this way, a godly mother not only saved her child; she was also able to raise him.

Pharaoh's daughter named the child Moses, but when he was grown, he refused to be known as the son of Pharaoh's daughter. Instead, he chose to be mistreated, along with the people of God, rather than enjoy the pleasure of sin for a short time. The book of Hebrews tells us that Moses regarded disgrace for the sake of Christ as of greater value than the treasures of Egypt, and he did it because he was looking ahead to his reward. He then left Egypt, not fearing the king's anger:

> *By faith he forsook Egypt, not fearing the wrath of the king; for he endured as seeing Him who is invisible.*   Hebrews 11:27

How did Moses persevere, being chased by the most powerful man on earth? He saw *"Him who is invisible."*

Why did Moses decline to be a prince and abandon even the potential of becoming king of Egypt? Why did he abandon the comfort, the power, the prestige, the popularity and the pleasure of the palace in Egypt? Why did he decide, instead, to suffer, be mistreated, be disgraced and be humiliated with his people — the Israelites? These are mind-boggling questions, especially to an ordinary person. Most people cannot understand why Moses would have made such a decision. Some say that it was foolish of him to give up his life in the palace. Yes, it may have seemed foolishness to men, but for Moses, it was the wisdom of God.

What was the reason Moses chose to be identified with his people? The answer is: *"for he looked to the reward."* What is a reward? It is something given after one has reached some achievement. And what was Moses' reward? It was seeing *"Him who is invisible."*

How could Moses have seen someone who was invisible? This is a paradox. He perceived the reality of God by faith. What is faith? The Bible says, *"Faith is being sure of what we hope for and certain of what we do not see"* (Hebrews 11:1, NIV). How did Moses get that kind of faith? Again, the Bible says, *"faith comes by hearing, and hearing by the word of God"* (Romans 10:17). It was apparent that Moses heard the Word of God from his mother who raised him. Although he was educated in all the wisdom of the Egyptians, the faith that his mother taught him was dominant in his thinking. For Moses, *"seeing Him who is invisible"* was far more valuable than enjoying the pleasures of sin temporarily at the palace, and suffering for Christ was greater riches than the treasures of Egypt.

Think of those missionaries I mentioned earlier in the book. They left all and served here in the Philippines for many years, suffering many things in the process. Just like Moses, they must have been motivated by something or Someone who was unseen.

The Bible says:

> *Eye has not seen, nor ear heard,*
> *Nor have entered into the heart of man*
> *The things which God has prepared for those who love Him.*
>
> 1 Corinthians 2:9

> *Therefore we do not lose heart. Even though our outward man is perishing, yet the inward man is being renewed day by day. For our light affliction, which is but for a moment, is working for us a far more exceeding and eternal weight of glory, while we do not look at the things which are seen, but at the things which are not seen. For the things which are seen are temporary, but the things which are not seen are eternal.*   1 Corinthians 4:16-18

THE TWO ADAMS

And so it is written, "The first man Adam became a living being." The last Adam became a life-giving spirit.

1 Corinthians 15:45

The Bible speaks of two Adams. Are they the same person? No! They are two different persons. What's the difference between the two? It is immense, very immense. It is the difference between Earth and Heaven.

The first man called Adam was created by God in His image and likeness. He was taken from the earth (terrestrial) and then formed and, finally, he was inbreathed by God. Thus, Adam became *"a living soul"* (Genesis 2:7). But this Adam, despite having been inbreathed by God, was mortal not immortal, as many Christians suggest and believe. His mortality was indicated by God when he was warned not to eat from the forbidden tree because if he did, he would surely die. Unfortunately, Adam disobeyed God, so the first Adam died, and the legacy that he left for the rest of mankind was one of death.

The second man called Adam was also said to be the *"last Adam."* He was God incarnate. He was none other than Jesus Christ, and

He was the *"express image"* of the invisible God (Hebrews 1:3). He was the Lord of Heaven (celestial). He is eternal and is a *"quickening [or life-giving] spirit."* He was the obedient Son of God who died on the cross to redeem us from the curse of sin and death. He rose again from the dead, to give all of us who believe in Him the hope of resurrection and immortality in Heaven.

What do these two Adams have to do with us today? Well, regarding the first Adam, we are stuck with his Adamic nature. As the saying goes, "We cannot choose our parents." We die like Adam, and we also face judgment and condemnation thereafter.

But, wait a minute! We can now choose and change our eternal destiny. That choice is in Jesus, *"the last Adam,"* who died to redeem us all from our sins and promised us all forgiveness of sins and eternal life. This is Good News indeed!

In the first Adam, we all die, but in the last Adam (Jesus Christ), we will live again. This is wonderful news!

Now, the big question is this: What will we do with Jesus Christ? If we ignore and reject Him, we will die in our sins without hope. This is why, in our evangelistic challenge to unsaved people and during our altar calls, we convince and persuade the lost that, besides turning away from sin, they should receive Jesus Christ as their personal Lord and Savior. Jesus Christ is indispensable to our salvation because there is *"no other name under heaven given among men by which we must be saved"* (Acts 4:12).

Yes, you can escape judgment and Hell right now. Repent and be sorry for your sins. Receive Jesus Christ into your heart, and your name will be written in the Book of Life in Heaven. Abide in Him, in His Word, the Bible, and in His Church. He is even now preparing us a place in Heaven, and He will come back to take us to Heaven to be with Him forever.

THE THREE DEATHS OF MAN

Therefore, just as through one man sin entered the world, and death through sin, and thus death spread to all men, because all sinned— (For until the law sin was in the world, but sin is not imputed when there is no law. Nevertheless death reigned from Adam to Moses, even over those who had not sinned according to the likeness of the transgression of Adam, who is a type of Him who was to come. But the free gift is not like the offense. For if by the one man's offense many died, much more the grace of God and the gift by the grace of the one Man, Jesus Christ, abounded to many.) Romans 5:12-15

As a consequence of Adam's disobedience, man began to die. The death contemplated in the Bible is of three kinds: namely, spiritual death, physical death and the second death.

WHAT IS DEATH?

What is death? Death is the absence of life. It is the cessation of all vital functions of physical life. It is the extinction and the end of man's existence on earth. There are some issues, however, with regards to this definition relative to the death of man. To give some clarification to this issue, it will help if we first know and understand the nature of man. Based on the psychological point of view, man is composed of two elements: body and soul. From the perspective of theologians, however, man is composed of three elements: spirit, soul and body. Both views are correct.

This analysis, or anatomy, of the nature of man is only for the purpose of knowing and understanding the complex structure and the interrelations of the elements of the human personality. Man is an integrated being. He is basically a body and soul and both of these human elements are an integral and essential part of man's existence. This means that one cannot survive without the other. When the word *body* is mentioned in the Bible, it is implied that the body has a soul. Conversely, when the word *soul* is mentioned, it is understood that this soul has a body. The life of the body is the soul, and when the body dies, the soul dies as well.

WHAT IS SPIRITUAL DEATH?

Now, what is spiritual death? It is the death of the spirit part of man. The spirit of man, in contradistinction to his soul, is his conscious connection with God. Man was complete when he was created by God, with spirit, soul and body. But when man sinned against God, his spirit died. Since then, men are spiritually dead, even if they are religious.

People who are without Christ are spiritual zombies; they are walking dead. That's why they need to be born again through faith in Christ, so that they can become spiritually alive again.

THE THREE DEATHS OF MAN

WHAT IS PHYSICAL DEATH?

How about physical death? This is the death which is commonly experienced by human beings, both sinners and saints (unbelievers or followers of Christ). Will there be people who will not experience this kind of death? The answer is yes. This is the exception to the rule that everybody dies. According to Paul, in 1 Thessalonians 4 and 1 Corinthians 15, those who are alive when Jesus Christ returns to earth *"will all be changed"* (1 Corinthians 15:51, NIV), apparently receiving glorified bodies, to join those who are resurrected to meet the Lord in the air and be with the Lord forever.

What happens to those who have died in Christ? Are they in Heaven now? No, not yet! Then where are they? They are in their graves. (RIP, Rest In Peace). Are they going to Heaven? Yes! When? At the Rapture, when Jesus Christ returns. They will be resurrected and will meet the Lord in the air to be forever with Him in Heaven.

WHAT IS THE SECOND DEATH?

How about those who have died without Christ? Are they in Hell now? No, not yet. Are they going to Hell? Definitely, yes. When? After the millennial reign of Jesus Christ, those who died without Him will be resurrected to face judgment. Then they will be thrown into the Lake of Fire, which is the *"second death"* (Revelation 20:14). This concept of death is rather extraordinary, peculiar and ironic compared with physical death. Whereas, in physical death, life (the body and soul) is ended, in the *"second death,"* life (the body and soul) is restored. For what purpose? Judgment in absentia is ruled out.

Proponents of the doctrine that the soul survives death misconstrue the meaning of Matthew 10:28, which says:

And do not fear those who kill the body but cannot kill the soul.
But rather fear Him who is able to destroy both soul and body in
hell.

This is one verse that proves that the human soul is mortal; it
can be killed. When I asked one pastor who is a proponent of an
immortal soul the question, What is killed in a body?, he could
not answer. It is because what is killed in a body is the soul that
gives life to that body. Therefore, when the body is killed, the soul
is also killed, and the result is physical death.

The first part of this verse which says, *"kill the body"* is presumed
to be a killing done by men. The second part of this verse which
says, *"kill the soul"* is the killing done by God. The latter part of
the verse has an eschatological dimension. This has reference to
the time of the Great White Throne Judgment, when sinners and
unbelievers will be thrown into the Lake of Fire. This is *"the second
death."* We can avoid this. Repent of your sins, and receive Jesus
Christ as your personal Lord and Savior, and you will be saved.

JUDGMENTS IN THE AFTERLIFE

And as it is appointed for men to die once, but after this the judgment.   Hebrews 9:27

The Bible tells us that there will be two judgments in the hereafter. They are (1) The Judgment Seat of Christ and (2) The Great White Throne Judgment.

Question: Will all the followers of Christ appear at the judgment? The answer is a yes, all Christians will appear before the Judgment Seat of Christ.

Will they be punished? Absolutely not!

Then why will they be judged? This judgment is not punitive; it is more of a rewards ceremony for those servants of God who have been faithful in serving Him while here on earth. Jesus said that we should *"lay up ... treasures in Heaven"* (Matthew 6:20) and not on earth because treasures in Heaven are lasting, while earthly treasures are temporary. I believe that the Judgment Seat of Christ will be the time when faithful servants of God will receive their rewards and the venue of this event is Heaven.

As the old saying goes:

Only one life, 'twill soon be past,
Only what's done for Christ will last. [1]

The things of this world will soon pass away,
But there is coming a judgment day.

The other judgment, the Great White Throne Judgment, will transpire after the millennial reign of Jesus Christ on earth. This will be the judgment for sinners, unbelievers and all liars. This judgment is punitive.

In his vision recorded in the book of Revelation, the apostle John saw the dead standing before God. They will be judged according to their works, which are all recorded in a book. Yes, God has a record book of the works of sinners and unbelievers.

Wait a minute! Why are these condemned dead standing before God to be judged? Isn't it true that the dead are nonexistent when they die? That's true! But they will also be resurrected to face judgment. This is consistent with what Jesus declared:

> *Do not marvel at this; for the hour is coming in which all who are in the graves will hear His voice and come forth — those who have done good, to the resurrection of life, and those who have done evil, to the resurrection of condemnation.*   John 5:28-29

This will be a dreadful scenario:

> *And anyone not found written in the Book of Life was cast into the lake of fire.*   Revelation 20:15

Actually, man is already judged while he is still alive, and the verdict is "GUILTY." According to the writings of Paul:

1. From the poem by C.T. Studd

174

For all have sinned and fall short of the glory of God.

Romans 3:23

For the wages of sin is death, but the gift of God is eternal life in Christ Jesus our Lord. Romans 6:23

Jesus said that those who do not believe in Him are *"condemned already"* (John 3:18) . But, while man is still alive, he has a chance to reverse the guilty verdict, be exonerated and escape punishment. How? As with our criminal justice system today, an accused person has a period after the Judge has already rendered judgment during which they can exhaust other available remedies. This period of time — usually about 15 days, depending on the case — is called, here in our country, a reglementary period. During that period, a person can appeal the decision of the judge. He still has potential remedies. But, if the accused is negligent and does not act in time, and the reglementary period is allowed to elapse, the judgment then becomes final and executory.

God has given man a lifetime reglementary period during which he can invoke the only remedy, and that is the substitutionary act of Christ on the cross of Calvary on our behalf. When a man dies without acting on or invoking the remedy, the judgment becomes final and executory, and there is no more remedy.

So, act now, while you are still alive. *"Now is the day of salvation"* (2 Corinthians 6:2). On your knees, repent of your sins. Open your heart and invite Jesus to come in. Then follow Him the rest of your life, and you will be saved!

Resurrections

Now if Christ is preached that He has been raised from the dead, how do some among you say that there is no resurrection of the dead? But if there is no resurrection of the dead, then Christ is not risen. And if Christ is not risen, then our preaching is empty and your faith is also empty. Yes, and we are found false witnesses of God, because we have testified of God that He raised up Christ, whom He did not raise up — if in fact the dead do not rise. For if the dead do not rise, then Christ is not risen. And if Christ is not risen, your faith is futile; you are still in your sins! Then also those who have fallen asleep in Christ have perished. If in this life only we have hope in Christ, we are of all men the most pitiable. But now Christ is risen from the dead, and has become the first-fruits of those who have fallen asleep. 1 Corinthians 15:12-20

The subject of the resurrection is essential to the Christian faith. All Christian practices would be futile without a belief in resurrection. Summing up all his arguments in defence of the resurrection, Paul concluded, *"If in this life only we have hope in Christ, we are of all men most miserable"* (KJV). This is how important the doctrine of resurrection is to every believer.

I am convinced that Paul expressed two of the most important quests of his lifetime when he wrote to the Philippian believers:

That I may know Him and the power of His resurrection.

Philippians 3:10

What is resurrection? It is the extraordinary bringing back to life of one who has been dead. It is the raising of the dead to life. This means that the body, which is resurrected, has become immortal and imperishable. This domain of power is exclusive to God alone.

Sometimes this word *resurrection* is misunderstood and inappropriately used as meaning resuscitation. Those who were brought back to life in the Bible were not resurrected but simply resuscitated. They died again later.

The resurrection of Jesus Christ is a historical fact that validates the Christians' belief in resurrection. His resurrection set a precedent. The evidence establishing the truth and the matter of fact of the resurrection of Jesus were undeniable, overwhelming and beyond any shadow of a doubt.

First, there is no argument that Jesus Christ died and was buried, just as the Bible says. This was corroborated by many witnesses. Then His resurrection was also affirmed by many eyewitnesses, including Peter and the other disciples, some women, more than five hundred other followers. Then he was also seen by Paul (see 1 Corinthians 15:5-8).

According to Jesus, there are two general resurrections. They are: (1) The resurrection to life and (2) The resurrection to damnation. This is in concurrence with the Old Testament prophecy of Daniel:

And many of those who sleep in the dust of the earth shall awake,
Some to everlasting life,
Some to shame and everlasting contempt.   Daniel 12:2

The time difference between these two resurrections is of eschatological dimensions. The first resurrection, which is the resurrection to life, is of several different phases. The resurrection of Jesus Christ is called the firstfruits. This will be followed by the Rapture, when those who have died in Christ will be resurrected at the Second Coming of Christ. Then, together with those Christians who are still alive and who will be changed in the twinkling of an eye during this unprecedented event in the history of mankind, they will meet the Lord in the air simultaneously, to be with Him in Heaven:

> *For the Lord Himself will descend from heaven with a shout, with the voice of an archangel, and with the trumpet of God. And the dead in Christ will rise first. Then we who are alive and remain shall be caught up together with them in the clouds to meet the Lord in the air. And thus we shall always be with the Lord.*
> 1 Thessalonians 4:16-17

Prior to the establishment of the millennial Kingdom of Jesus Christ, there will be Tribulation saints and the two witnesses, among others, who will also be resurrected.

The second general resurrection, which is the resurrection to damnation, will take place after the millennial Kingdom of Jesus Christ:

> *But the rest of the dead did not live again until the thousand years were finished.*
> Revelation 20:5

The purpose of this second resurrection is for the unbelieving to face judgment. Afterward, they will be cast into the Lake of Fire.

We can escape this dreadful Lake of Fire, and this is the Good News. Through faith in Jesus Christ, we will be spared and, instead, be included among those who will be in the first resurrection. Repent of your sins today and receive Jesus Christ as your personal Lord and Savior, and you will be saved. Live for God, and whether you live or die, you have the assurance of salvation!

CHANGING OUR OWN WORLD

The word which came to Jeremiah from the LORD*, saying: "Arise and go down to the potter's house, and there I will cause you to hear My words." Then I went down to the potter's house, and there he was, making something at the wheel. And the vessel that he made of clay was marred in the hand of the potter; so he made it again into another vessel, as it seemed good to the potter to make.*   Jeremiah 18:1-4

God told the prophet Jeremiah to go down to the local potter's house, and there He would give him His message. So, he went, and there he saw the potter working at the wheel. The vessel the potter was shaping from the clay was marred in his hands, so he turned it into another vessel, shaping it as seemed best to him.

Perhaps you and I can relate to and identify with the story of the vessel in the potter's hand before and after our conversion to Christ. Before Christ came into our lives, we were like this vessel which was *"marred."* The word *marred* denotes that something was wrong with the vessel, even as the potter was shaping it from the clay. Maybe a foreign object got into the clay and contaminated it. That would compromise and alter the outcome.

180

The potter's intention was for the vessel to be perfect. The potter here is God, and we are that vessel. He shaped us:

And the LORD God formed man of the dust of the ground, and breathed into his nostrils the breath of life; and man became a living being. Genesis 2:7

So, when we think about the potter Jeremiah encountered and his intentions for the vessel he was shaping, our minds go back to the dawn of Creation. After God created man, His evaluation of him was no less than perfect. He declared His creation, man, to be *"very good"*:

Then God saw everything that He had made, and indeed it was very good. Genesis 1:31

Before Christ came into my life, I was like that marred vessel. My life was broken, shattered and fragmented. My wife and I were separated, and it was all my fault. I was being controlled by an irresistible force called *sin.*

I even contemplated ending my life. Before that happened, thank God, two Filipina lady missionaries witnessed to me about the Gospel of Jesus Christ. I repented of my sins and accepted Jesus into my life, as my Lord and Savior.

When I told my wife about my conversion experience with Christ, she also believed, and we were reconciled. Praise God! Hallelujah! As our gratitude to God, we both entered the Bible school in preparation for our commitment and dedication to serve God.

After our graduation from Bible school, my wife and I, as a team, traveled to many provinces of the Philippines preaching and sharing the Gospel of Jesus Christ in schools, plazas and churches.

Eventually, when our family had grown, we settled for the more stationary ministry of church establishment and pastoring. Until now, we have established four congregations.

Then God sent us some wonderful Swedish partners, and with their help our work expanded to social, relief and educational ministries by putting up pre-school, elementary and high schools. Today we have more than two thousand children studying in our two schools in Taytay and Infanta. The purpose of these schools is to help provide quality and affordable basic education to the children of poor families, especially those living in the poor colonies. Since we put up these schools, more than 80,000 children have studied there, and more than 13,000 of those graduated. Many of them are now professionals in their own fields of endeavor.

A well-known story goes like this: a pastor was studying his Bible one Saturday morning, preparing his message to the church the following day. His wife opened the door of the room where he was studying and said to him, "Honey, can you please look after Junior (their son who was about six years old) because I'm going to the market to buy food."

The pastor had not yet finished preparing his message, so he tried to think of some game that might keep Junior occupied while he continued his studies. He noticed a world map on the wall, and an idea came to him. Taking it down, he showed it to Junior and said, "Let's play a game, son. I will tear this world map in pieces, and you go into the other room and see if you can put it back together again. Okay?"

"Okay, Papa," Junior answered.

The pastor thought it would take his son at least an hour to get the map back together, and that would give him sufficient time to finish his preparations. After only ten minutes, there was a knock on the door. He was sure his wife could not be back from the market so soon, as it was quite a distance away. When he opened the door, he was amazed to see his son standing there proudly holding the completed world map. "Wow! How did you do that so fast, son?" he asked.

Junior answered, "While you were tearing up the map of the world, I saw a figure of a man at the back of the map. I don't know much about the world, but I know the parts of a man — where to put his head, his hands and his feet. So, I figured out that if I could make the man all right, his world would also be all right!"

"Oh, you are so right, Junior," his father said. "You have just given me the message for tomorrow."

Yes, before Jesus came, man was not right, and his world was not right either. That's why Jesus said:

"Come to Me, all you who labor and are heavy laden, and I will give you rest. Take My yoke upon you and learn from Me, for I am gentle and lowly in heart, and you will find rest for your souls. For My yoke is easy and My burden is light."
Matthew 11:28-30

The apostle Paul added to this:

Therefore, if anyone is in Christ, he is a new creation; old things have passed away; behold, all things have become new.
2 Corinthians 5:17

This change in our lives, effected by our faith in the Lord Jesus Christ, has a ripple effect in the water of humanity. Our salvation has an impact and an influence upon the people around us that will also result in change to their lives.

BLESSED ARE THE POOR

Christians are catalysts, which means they are agents for change — God's agents for change. If Christians are committed, dedicated and obedient to the will of God, they can become instruments of change for the better.

We may not be able to change the whole world, but we can surely change our own world. Hallelujah! The best is yet to come! Glory to God! Praise His holy name!

LOVE SUBLIME

Jesus said to him, " 'You shall love the Lord your God with all your heart, with all your soul, and with all your mind.' This is the first and great commandment. And the second is like it: 'You shall love your neighbor as yourself.' On these two commandments hang all the Law and the Prophets." Matthew 22:37-40

This divine dictum was the answer of our Lord Jesus Christ to the question of one of the teachers of the Law regarding the most important of all the commandments. This, therefore, is the highest of all the Christian's morals imperatives.

Jesus quoted the ten commandments in a capsulated compendium, plus one. What is this "plus one?" It is to "love ourselves," after loving God and our neighbors. This was not included in the original Ten Commandments. So, for Christians, we might say, there are now eleven commandments.

The question of the teacher of the Law relative to this issue was rather interesting. Apparently he just wanted to follow one of the Ten Commandments, and that was why he asked which one was the most important. But the decalogue is essentially a unit, meaning to say, one commandment cannot be separated from the rest of the commandments. They are integrated just like the human soul that cannot be separated from the human body, even by physical death.

Now, the big question is this: As Christians, are we still obligated to follow or obey the decalogue? The answer is yes, plus one. This responsibility was not abrogated, even though we are now under grace and no more under the Law. We are to follow this divine dictum, not to be saved, because we are already saved through faith in the Lord Jesus Christ. We follow the Decalogue plus one because this is our code of conduct, our standard of Christian and personal behavior based on this moral principle. It is characteristic of a Christian to love God, his fellow being and himself.

When, why and how do we love God? Our love affair with God begins when we are saved and have been born again. We love God because He first loved us. It is a reciprocal and mutual love relationship between God and man that develops when man is saved. And how should we love God? Answer: with all of our heart, soul, mind and strength.

The Israelites were reminded by God of this divine dictum and told that they should pass it on to their children as a legacy of faith. It should be part of a majority of their conversations. As a symbol of their love and obedience to God, they were to tie these commandments to their foreheads and arms (see Deuteronomy 6).

The Jewish concept of the heart and mind is that the two are integrated. For example:

For as he thinks in his heart, so is he.   Proverbs 23:7

The two can, however, be distinguished by way of rhetorical function. This means that man's love of God must involve his total being, both his abstract and physical elements.

186

A closer look at this divine dictum will reveal that when God gave it to His people, the Israelites, and when Jesus pronounced it, both were in the imperative mode. This means that the commandments were mandates, not options. When God says something to His people and then He repeats it, we'd better pay attention. This is much more true when He repeats it three times. In that case, we can know that it is something very serious indeed.

As parents, when we discipline our children over some of their misbehaviors, we sometimes warn them by counting: one, two, three. After three, if they have not listened, then they get the corresponding punishment.

How do we love God with our whole being? The first mention is loving God with all our heart. The human heart is the seat of emotion. We get emotional when we are in love. It is an exciting, powerful and wonderful feeling. Someone in love will defy reason, ignore ridicule and suffer all sorts of mistreatment just to be with the person they beloved. It is a feeling of "you and me against the world."

Do we love God like that? Do we get emotional with our love for Him? I do. Every time I think of how Jesus Christ suffered on the cross to redeem me and save me from my sins, I get emotional — very emotional. Tears run freely down my cheeks. Every time I remember how God lifted me up from a life of poverty to a life of plenty, I burst into tears, just thinking about God's goodness and faithfulness to me and my family. Every time I worship God in church, lifting up my hands and singing songs of praise to Him, I get emotional. This emotion is the expression of my love for God, and I know full well what I am doing because my mind tells me so. My love of God is with ardent and fervent dedication, devotion and obedience to His will.

The next question is: How do we love our fellow being? Aside from the profound illustration given by our Lord Jesus Christ in answer to the question by one expert of the Law, *"And who is my neighbor?"*(Luke 10:29), the apostle Paul gave a wonderful exposition and elaboration on this subject of sublime love (see 1 Corinthians 13). This love emanates from God, for *"God is love"* (1 John 4:8 and 16).

Love for our neighbor is characterized by patience and kindness and an absence of envy, pride, rudeness or selfishness. Godly love is *"not easily angered,"* and *"keeps no record of wrongs"* (1 Corinthians 13:5, NIV). It *"does not delight in evil but rejoices with the truth"* (verse 6). *"It always protects, always trusts, always hopes, always perseveres"* (verse 7). *"Love never fails"* (verse 8).

One of the characteristics of love is sacrifice. God loves us so much that He sacrificed His own Son. Sacrifice is the act of offering someone or something precious to God or to someone else. To sacrifice also means "to surrender or give up at a loss" or "to endure." We all know that Jesus Christ did this when He suffered on the cross. This was a cruel love, and sometimes love can be cruel. Jesus said:

> *If anyone desires to come after Me, let him deny himself, and take up his cross, and follow Me.*   Matthew 16:24

Does this mean that we have to take up a literal wooden cross and carry it around? I have seen some Christians do that. But I believe that the meaning of what Jesus said is part of the Divine Dictum we are considering here. It demands our love for God and our fellow being, and when we do love in this way, we deny ourselves. The direction of this act of love is vertical, toward God, and the other is horizontal, toward our fellow being. The image formed in this act of love is a cross.

Of course, we must not neglect or ignore to love ourselves. This is the eleventh commandment, according to our Lord Jesus

Christ. In one sense, it is human nature that everyone loves himself or herself, so I need not elaborate on this point, but many hate themselves.

Also, the order or sequence of our loves is very important. It must be: first, love Jesus, then love others, and then yourself. That is:

Jesus
Others
Yourself

This spells JOY, which is constant happiness, whether the circumstances in our lives are good or bad. Yes, love sublime will bring you joy unspeakable and full of glory!

THE CHRISTIANS' VIEW AND VALUE OF WORK

And on the seventh day God ended His work which He had done, and He rested on the seventh day from all His work which He had done. Then God blessed the seventh day and sanctified it, because in it He rested from all His work which God had created and made.
Genesis 2:2-3

Work occupies at least a third of our lifetime. In each day, we allocate eight hours to work, eight hours to sleep and eight hours to leisure or recreation.

To many people, work is a boring routine and a drudgery of activity, but to others, especially Christians, work is an essential and significant part and purpose of our life. Through our work (some call it a job), we help support ourselves and sustain our families, render service to others and our society, to our government and, ultimately, to God. Besides, work gives a person a sense of dignity, fulfillment, self-esteem and financial and economic security.

There are different kinds of work and many varied areas of endeavor. There are, for example, those who are engaged in agricultural work (farmers), in industrial work (factory workers), in commercial and business work, in construction, in transportation, in maritime work (seamen), in medical work, in the legal profession, in church work, in government, in education etc. There are those whose work involves mostly mental exertion and others whose work requires manual labor.

There are those who are involved in what we consider to be dirty work, like garbage collecting, sewage control and sanitation management. Although these dirty and stinky manual jobs seem to some to be demeaning to the workers, we must be very thankful to those who maintain the hygiene of our towns and cities. Without sanitation workers, we would be vulnerable to outbreaks and epidemics of all sorts of sicknesses and diseases in our communities.

How do we render services to others through our work? Through the goods and services we produce. Other people are benefited, and this adds to the compensation we receive, which helps with the sustenance of ourselves and our family.

Let's take the example of farmers. What they produce not only feeds their own family but also many others. Another example would be those who are involved in the construction industry. We have infrastructures like roads, bridges and buildings in our communities and cities because of construction workers. We all benefit from their labors.

Also the taxes derived from the sale of the many goods and services provided serve as funds to finance our government systems. In this way, our individual and corporate work contributes to the stability, sustainability, symbiosis and dynamics of our society and its government.

God is a worker, and when He created man, He intended for him to become a worker also. The Divine imprint in man, who is created in the image and likeness of God, suggests and implies this intention and purpose.

Who can doubt that God is a worker? He worked six days in creating the universe and all that is in it, and He wants man to be a worker, too, a partner in work that is.

> Then the LORD God took the man and put him in the garden of Eden to tend and keep it.   Genesis 2:15

God wants man to be like Him, to be active, creative and productive. Contrary to the belief of many that work is part of the curse, here we see that before the fall, work had already been instituted by God for man. God provided nature through His creation, but He placed man to be the cultivator of that nature, and so work has become the cultural mandate for man.

It is God who provides the land, the seed and growth to that seed, but it is man who has to do the work of cultivating, sowing and reaping. God gives life to the fetus in the mother's womb, but when the baby is born, it is the mother's responsibility to look after that baby. A doctor puts a bandage on the wound of a patient, but it is God who does the healing. This is a universal working partnership principle between God and man.

Understanding the essence and significance of work and seeing our work as our human cultural mandate will make our work satisfactory and never a drudgery, even though it may be a routine activity. God was satisfied with His work. After He saw all that He had made, He said, "*It was very good*" (Genesis 1:31). We should mimic this kind of work attitude. We should take satisfaction from our work.

This is what I do personally. I am satisfied with my work. In fact, I enjoy it. When we have this kind of work attitude, our work will never be boring or seem like a drudgery of activity.

Many workers, including Christian workers, frequently change jobs. Usually it is because they are not satisfied either with their work or their salary (although there may be other reasons). God has promised His people that if they are fully obedient to Him, He will make them the head and not the tail (see Deuteronomy 28:13), but sometimes we have to start at the tail and work our way up to becoming the head. But if we keep jumping from one job to another because we hate work, without spending enough time in any one position, we are doomed to always remain the tail and can never be the head.

There are rules, serious rules, in the New Testament governing our Christian work attitude. They are tantamount to Christian Work Ethics. First, there is this rule which says:

If anyone will not work, neither shall he eat. 2 Thessalonians 3:10

This is clearly an injunction against lazy Christians. Paul rebuked the lazy among the Thessalonians for being idle and going around depending on other Christians for their sustenance, although they were quite capable of working. That entire passage is worth quoting:

But we command you, brethren, in the name of our Lord Jesus Christ, that you withdraw from every brother who walks disorderly and not according to the tradition which he received from us. For you yourselves know how you ought to follow us, for we were not disorderly among you; nor did we eat anyone's bread free of charge, but worked with labor and toil night and day, that we might not be a burden to any of you, not because we do not have authority, but to make ourselves an example of how you should follow us.

For even when we were with you, we commanded you this: If anyone will not work, neither shall he eat. For we hear that there

193

are some who walk among you in a disorderly manner, not work-
ing at all, but are busybodies. Now those who are such we com-
mand and exhort through our Lord Jesus Christ that they work
in quietness and eat their own bread.   2 Thessalonians 3:6-12

Paul also warned the Philippian Christians not to gain their income from illicit means, and he taught them to share with those who had genuine needs.

With every rule, there is an exception. Who are those exempt from work? Children, for one, should be exempt from work so that they can go to school and learn. They also require time for play if they are to develop properly. Parents should work and support their growing children.

The elderly, especially the weak and the sick, are also exempt from work, so their children should look after their well-being. This charitable work toward the elderly is consistent with the biblical admonition to children:

Honor your father and your mother, that your days may be long
upon the land which the LORD your God is giving you.
Exodus 20:11

Yes, it's payback time. They supported you, and now it's your turn to support them.

We must be thankful to God if we have work, and we must do our job without complaining and murmuring. And, finally, what-ever we do, let us do it all for His glory:

Do all things without complaining and disputing, that you may
become blameless and harmless, children of God without fault in
the midst of a crooked and perverse generation, among whom you

194

*shine as lights in the world, holding fast the word of life, so that
I may rejoice in the day of Christ that I have not run in vain or
labored in vain.* Philippians 2:14-16

What does it mean for us to do our jobs without complaining or
murmuring? These usually occur when we are dissatisfied with
our work. It may have to do with our working conditions, with
the attitude of our superiors or with our compensation. Instead of
rebelling against an employer or reviling them, it is better to just
quietly resign and look for another job.

As Christians, we have another consideration: We must keep
intact and protect our Christian testimony, our integrity and our
conviction, sometimes under very difficult circumstances. We
must always find ways to glorify God with our work. Then, just
as God rested after six days of work, we must rest, and we must
honor God on the seventh day by going to His House, the church.
In church, we Christians acknowledge the blessings and favor of
God over the past days and express thanks through worship and
thanksgiving. This includes the giving of our tithes and offerings.

The pattern was set by God Himself. For six days He labored,
and then He rested on the seventh day. This mandate to God's
people has not been abrogated; it still stands and is in effect. Obedience to this mandate has nothing to do with our salvation because
we have been saved through faith in Christ Jesus, but it is still a
matter of obligation. Don't be an ingrate! God gave us life, salvation, strength, sound mind, resources and work opportunities, so
we owe Him a lot. Glorify God in your work, and then go to His
House to give Him thanks.

TRAGIC LOVE

*Then the children of Israel did evil in the sight of the LORD, and
served the Baals.*   Judges 2:11

*So the children of Israel did evil in the sight of the LORD. They
forgot the LORD their God, and served the Baals and Asherahs.*
                                                              Judges 3:7

*When Ehud was dead, the children of Israel again did evil in the
sight of the LORD.*   Judges 4:1

*Then the children of Israel did evil in the sight of the LORD. So
the LORD delivered them into the hand of Midian for seven years.*
                                                              Judges 6:1

This phrase, *"the children of Israel did evil in the sight of the LORD,"*
as you can see, is repeated several times in the book of Judges.
What was this evil that provoked the Lord to anger against His
people? They forsook and forgot the Lord, the God of their fathers,
who had brought them out of Egypt. What was worse: they followed and worshipped various gods of the people around them,

like Baal and the Astoreths. Why were they always backsliding in this way? It was because these were new generation of Israelites who had come along after the death of Joshua, and they did not know the Lord or the great things He had done for their nation.

Because these new generations refused to give up their evil practices and stubborn ways, God allowed the enemies surrounding them, like the Philistines, to afflict and oppress them. When they cried out to the Lord because of their afflictions at the hand of these oppressive enemies, the Lord had compassion on them and raised up deliverers who set therm free again. These deliverers were also called judges, and they were men and women who knew God, and He was with them and often gave them extraordinary powers.

God had warned the Israelites before they entered into Canaan, the land of promise, not to follow other gods, the gods of the people around them. They were also precluded from intermarrying with the people of Canaan. They must not give their daughters to the sons of Canaan or take Canaanite daughters for their sons. Why? Because the daughter of Canaan would turn away their sons from following the Lord to serve other gods, and the Lord's anger would burn against them as a result.

Samson was among these godly judges and deliverers whom the Lord gave to the Israelites when they cried out to Him by reason of the oppression of their enemies. Samson was an extraordinary man. He had lived under the vow of a Nazarite from birth. This special vow was for the purpose of separating oneself unto the Lord. A Nazarite must abstain from wine and other fermented drink. He must not go near a dead body, and during the entire period of his vow, no razor could be used on his head. He must let his hair grow. But, alas, this man's life was also a reflection and representation of the condition and moral reality of the nation of Israel during this period. Samson had his ups and his downs.

Samson had supernatural strength. Where did that strength come from? Some say that it came from his long hair, but others say that his strength came from the Lord, when His Spirit came upon Samson in power. Personally, I think the two are related.

At one point, Samson killed a young lion with his bare hands. With a jawbone of a donkey, he killed a thousand of the Philistines. It seemed that Samson was invincible against his Philistine enemies. But he did have one weakness, and that weakness proved to be his undoing. He loved women, especially, it seems, Philistine women.

One day, Samson saw a young Philistine woman in Timnah, and he wanted her. When he returned home, he said to his parents, *"I have seen a woman in Timnah of the daughters of the Philistines; now therefore, get her for me as a wife"* (Judges 14:2).

His parents objected: *"Is there no woman among the daughters of your brethren, or among all my people, that you must go and get a wife from the uncircumcised Philistines?"* (verse 3).

Samson remained unmoved. He was convinced that this was the right woman for him. *"Get her for me, for she pleases me well"* (verse 3).

Who was right? Samson or his parents? The Bible states emphatically:

Children, obey your parents in the Lord, for this is right.
Ephesians 6:1

It doesn't say that parents are always right, but it says that it is always right to obey your parents. The book of Proverbs teaches:

There is a way that seems right to a man,
But its end is the way of death.　　　　　　　Proverbs 14:12

Sure enough, Samson's marriage to the Philistine woman ended in tragedy. She and her father were burned to death by the Philistines, and Samson had to flee from his enemies.

But Samson didn't learn his lesson. Now he went to Gaza and slept with a prostitute, further lowering his standards and his taste in women. He always seemed to be in the wrong place at a wrong time.

Next, he fell in love with a woman named Delilah. This woman was not only dangerous; she was treacherous. She didn't love Samson; she was just after his money. What was worse: she was in cahoots with the Philistines to learn where his real strength lay.

When she nagged him incessantly, Samson finally gave in and told Delilah that if his hair was cut, he would become as weak as any other man. The next thing he knew he was waking up, and his head had been shaved while he was sleeping. He wasn't concerned, convinced that he could escape as before. This time, however, it was different:

So he awoke from his sleep, and said, "I will go out as before, at other times, and shake myself free!" But he did not know that the LORD had departed from him.   Judges 16:20

What happened to Samson next is very sad:

Then the Philistines took him and put out his eyes, and brought him down to Gaza. They bound him with bronze fetters, and he became a grinder in the prison.   Verse 21

Now Samson was forced to get serious. With extreme remorse, he prayed to God to once more restore to him his supernatural strength in order to exact revenge against his Philistine enemies. God heard that plea:

> And Samson took hold of the two middle pillars which supported the temple, and he braced himself against them, one on his right and the other on his left. Then Samson said, "Let me die with the Philistines!" And he pushed with all his might, and the temple fell on the Lords and all the people who were in it. So the dead that he killed at his death were more than he had killed in his life.
>
> Verses 29-30

At the end of his life, Samson met tragedy, and it was all his fault. What was the cause of this tragedy? It was love, the love of women who don't belong to the same community of faith. Love's story is supposed to end with the words *happily ever after*, not with such tragedy.

This is a serious warning to all Christians, both men and women, but especially to those who are single. If you don't want your love life to turn to tragedy, don't be yoked together with unbelievers:

> Do not be unequally yoked together with unbelievers. For what fellowship has righteousness with lawlessness? And what communion has light with darkness? And what accord has Christ with Belial? Or what part has a believer with an unbeliever? And what agreement has the temple of God with idols? For you are the temple of the living God. As God has said:
>
> "I will dwell in them
> And walk among them.
> I will be their God,
> And they shall be My people."

Therefore

"Come out from among them
And be separate, says the Lord.
Do not touch what is unclean,
And I will receive you.
I will be a Father to you,
And you shall be My sons and daughters,
Says the Lord Almighty."   2 Corinthians 6:14-18

Save yourself from tremendous trouble and tragedy. Don't become romantically involved with unbelievers.

A CHRISTIAN'S PERSONAL PERSPECTIVE

Brethren, I do not count myself to have apprehended; but one thing I do, forgetting those things which are behind and reaching forward to those things which are ahead, I press toward the goal for the prize of the upward call of God in Christ Jesus.

Philippians 3:13-14

At the end of each year, many evaluate their achievements during the past year and assess what they should do in the coming year. Then, they make a "New Year's resolution." In this way, they hope to avoid the mistakes and blunders they committed in the past. In fact, they resolve not to repeat them. Through the mistakes of the past, some have learned valuable, albeit expensive, lessons that will make them more cautious in the days ahead.

Some have health issues and may want to slow down on their food intake and discipline their bodies to do more exercise. These are commendable resolutions.

For most of us, New Years is always a good time to save more money and prioritize our expenses and purchases so as to have more left over for the emergencies of life. These are all good and beneficial to us, if we are committed to resolve our personal issues.

But what about our Christian life and testimony? Do we have personal issues that we need to resolve in the new year? How will we tackle these issues? What are our priorities as Christians, whether we work in the sacred or in the secular? To answer these questions, I would like to adopt Paul's perspective on his personal life and service to God. He said, *"One thing I do, forgetting those things which are behind and reaching forward to those things which are ahead, I press toward the goal for the prize of the upward call of God in Christ Jesus."* What was he talking about? He was talking about the hindsight, the insight and the foresight of his life and service to God as a Christian. He was focused on doing *"one thing,"* and that one thing was forgetting the past and reaching out for the future.

What were the things that Paul was forgetting? I believe that he was referring to his zeal for his former religion. Paul, just like so many people, had been sincere, but he was sincerely wrong. He declared:

> *But what things were gain to me, these I have counted loss for Christ. Yet indeed I also count all things loss for the excellence of the knowledge of Christ Jesus my Lord, for whom I have suffered the loss of all things, and count them as rubbish, that I may gain Christ and be found in Him, not having my own righteousness, which is from the law, but that which is through faith in Christ, the righteousness which is from God by faith; that I may know Him and the power of His resurrection, and the fellowship of His sufferings, being conformed to His death, if, by any means, I may attain to the resurrection from the dead.* Philippians 3:7-11

Using commercial terms, Paul had thought that he had profit or gain from his former religion and activities, but when he met and came to know Christ Jesus, what he had thought was gain now became *"loss"* for him and worthless compared with the majesty of the knowledge of Christ. He had thought that he had righteousness by the Law, but that was insufficient and insignificant compared with the righteousness by faith in Christ Jesus. In fact, now he treated all those past things as *"rubbish."* The King James Version of the Bible translates this word as *"dung,"* which means "manure." That's about as worthless as you can get.

What did Paul mean by *"forgetting"* past things? He meant that past things must not influence or affect our present and future Christian life. I have heard many Christians, when they testify, seem to magnify their past above their present life in Christ. They revel in the fact that were murderers, rapists, robbers, swindlers or drug addicts. I believe that this is unnecessary and inappropriate. Sometimes it is scary to get close to such people. You never know if there might be a recurrence of their former life.

We believe that Christians should not tell a lie, but we also don't have to tell all the gory details of our past lives. There are good truths, and there are bad truths. We don't have to tell the bad truths, especially when they are self-incriminating and will besmirch our name and our family's reputation. No one is asking anyway, and we're not under oath in a court of law. I believe that our sinful past has been covered and erased by the precious blood of Jesus Christ. That is enough to know.

What is the "one thing" that we should be focused on doing with each new year? The answer to this question is a serious challenge to Christians, especially to Christian workers. I always advise and encourage my fellow pastors to focus on their work. We must not compromise our commitment, dedication and devotion to God and His calling for us with the things of this world. We need things in order to exist, but our priority must be to pursue God and be faithful in His service.

I have often received invitations to speak outside of our church, but if they conflict with our church services, I decline them because I am committed to serving our congregation. I must be loyal to that commitment.

As I have outlined in the story part of the book, during the early years of our ministry, I was a very poor pastor, and most of our members were also poor because they came from a squatters colony. Many times I was forced to do some moonlighting in order augment our income and feed my wife and three children. I did not like to squeeze our members for money because they were poor too, so I bought and sold items of clothing and cars.

Then I discovered how to be financially stable through the economic principles espoused by Joseph in the Bible. As a result, with capital gathered through years of savings (and loans I was able to secure) I ventured into some real estate transactions. I was able to acquire two properties and built two houses, and that set me on a course of action. I was about to get seriously into buying land, building houses and selling those houses when suddenly I realized that this business was sucking me out of the ministry. My focus had been diverted from ministry to business. The result was that I quit the business and refocused on my pastoral ministry.

Let us remember as the song says:

Only one life, it will soon be past,
Only what's done for Christ will last.
Things in this world will soon pass away
And there is coming a judgment day.

Jesus said:

For what will it profit a man if he gains the whole world, and loses his own soul?   Mark 8:36

But seek first the kingdom of God and His righteousness, and all these things shall be added to you.   Matthew 6:33

Since I refocused my life in pursuit of and service to God, I haven't had to worry about our sustenance, shelter, education for our children and money for whatever else we needed, because He promised:

And my God shall supply all your need according to His riches in glory by Christ Jesus.   Philippians 4:19

Praise God! Hallelujah!

CREDULOUS CHRISTIANS

And Jesus answered and said to them: "Take heed that no one deceives you.   Matthew 24:4

I would like to issue a stern warning to honest and sincere Christians around the world to be discreet and discerning about what they read on Facebook and other social media, especially concerning Christian doctrines. Not all messages, pronouncements and declarations of preachers, pastors and ministers of the Gospel are the Word of God (the Truth). Some of them are nonsense bordering on ignorance (at least of the Scriptures) and stupidity. As messengers of God, we have a moral imperative to speak the truth in love, and the Bible is the paragon of truth.

Not long ago, a well known preacher from the U.S. posted on Facebook in big and bold letters: YOU'RE FULL OF RESURRECTION POWER. Does this preacher know what he is talking about? If he knows, he's in trouble because this is a blatant lie.

It is also usurpation, meaning claiming power and authority that do not belong to him. Resurrection power is exclusive to God, so that preacher is treading on forbidden territory. This is the domain of the divine, so it seems that he is playing God.

The sad and tragic part is that thousands of sincere and honest Christians around the world will believe him and like his post, thus saying, "Amen!" This means that they concur and conform to his declaration that Christians possess, not only resurrection power, but full resurrection power. How can Christians be so gullible as to be duped into believing such a lie? The answer is: because many Christians are ignorant of the Scriptures. Consequently, they are not thinking correctly. They may be sincere, but they are sincerely wrong.

RAISED OR RESURRECTED?

Then, behold, the veil of the temple was torn in two from top to bottom; and the earth quaked, and the rocks were split, and the graves were opened; and many bodies of the saints who had fallen asleep were raised; and coming out of the graves after His resurrection, they went into the holy city and appeared to many.

Matthew 27:51-53

The astonishing events described in this passage are not easy to interpret in the light other scriptures. Interestingly enough, this incident is only found in the book of Matthew and not in the other gospel accounts. According to these verses, many bodies of dead saints (still Old Testament?) rose from their graves after the resurrection of Jesus. Then they went into the Holy City and appeared to many. The big question is: were these dead saints resurrected together with Jesus? Or were they merely raised to life? There is no question as to the resurrection of Jesus because it is a given. That others rose in the same way is highly questionable.

I have always maintained the position that all dead saints — whether Old Testament or New Testament — will be resurrected at the time of the Rapture, when Jesus returns. Is this event a biblical discrepancy? One of the challenges pastors, Bible teachers and all preachers face is to be able to reconcile the controversial and seemingly contradictory verses and passages of the Bible so that we can arrive at a unity of belief about the Scriptures. This can be achieved by means of sound and correct interpretation.

So, how do we answer this question? First, let's look at the meaning of the word *resurrection* and its implications. The apostle Paul had a rather comprehensive meaning of the word, one that presupposes, as a rule, that one has already died. It is also a condition precedent to go to Heaven. When someone is resurrected, there are substantial changes in their nature, especially in their body. Paul used the metaphor of a seed sown into the ground to illustrate these changes:

> *So also is the resurrection of the dead. The body is sown in corruption, it is raised in incorruption. It is sown in dishonor, it is raised in glory. It is sown in weakness, it is raised in power. It is sown a natural body, it is raised a spiritual body.*
>
> 1 Corinthians 15:42-44

A resurrected body will be an immortal body, one that will never die. Therefore, the saints of old mentioned in Matthew 27:52-53 were not resurrected. Instead, they were simply raised to life again.

The Bible is silent about whether or not these people went to Heaven afterward. What, then, happened to them? They died again. All of the individuals who died and were then raised to life by the power of God eventually died again. This includes Lazarus, the dear friend whom Jesus raised to life. These, too, await the Rapture in order to be resurrected when Jesus returns.

THE REMEDY OF REDEMPTION

So when the woman saw that the tree was good for food, that it was pleasant to the eyes, and a tree desirable to make one wise, she took of its fruit and ate. She also gave to her husband with her, and he ate. Then the eyes of both of them were opened, and they knew that they were naked; and they sewed fig leaves together and made themselves coverings.

*And they heard the sound of the L*ORD *God walking in the garden in the cool of the day, and Adam and his wife hid themselves from the presence of the L*ORD *God among the trees of the garden.*

*Then the L*ORD *God called to Adam and said to him, "Where are you?"*

So he said, "I heard Your voice in the garden, and I was afraid because I was naked; and I hid myself."

And He said, "Who told you that you were naked? Have you eaten from the tree of which I commanded you that you should not eat?"

Then the man said, "The woman whom You gave to be with me, she gave me of the tree, and I ate."   Genesis 3:6-12

The ramifications of Adam's disobedience in the Garden of Eden were direct and collateral. His offence brought death to himself and also to the rest of mankind. Besides that, it brought destruction, damage and hostility, undermining the harmony of God's created order.

Adding to this sad and tragic episode of the human and divine drama was the behind-the-scenes divine trauma. I believe (I can only conjecture or speculate) that God was deeply hurt by this horrendous act of Adam. God is also an emotional God. At one time He said, *"I am a jealous God"* (Exodus 20:5). Others have called the offence of Adam "treason" or "a crime." Most theologians call it sin, but I call it betrayal. After all that God had done for Adam — He gave him life, gave him love and fellowship, gave him the Garden of Eden and gave him Eve — the man betrayed Him. This, of course, was caused by the Intruder, the devil, who did nothing good for Adam and Eve, but lied to them, and they believed him and not God.

Do you know how it feels to be betrayed? Ask a husband whose wife has given her body to another man. Ask a pastor about members who have left him and gone to a mega-church. Can we ask God how He felt when He was betrayed by Adam? Of course you can, but I'm not sure if you will get an answer. When we are betrayed, we feel humiliated and rejected. It's a very painful feeling.

Let's look at Adam's side of the story. There was tremendous tension created when Eve offered him the forbidden fruit and asked him to eat it. He was in a dilemma. If he refused to eat the forbidden fruit, he might lose Eve, and he didn't want to be alone and lonely or unhappy as before. So, he decided to take a bite and die with Eve instead.

But what did Adam really do that day? He was being selfish. He was only thinking of himself. He was not thinking this thing through to its logical conclusion. He had allowed his emotions to overrule his reason. And that was the source of all of human misery. Blame it on Adam, folks.

For his part, Adam passed the blame along to Eve, and Eve blamed the serpent. This is what we have come to call "the blame game." Doesn't it sounds typical of people even today? This was, as a matter of fact, a love story and a love triangle — Adam's love for God pitted against his love for Eve.

God is a God of love, but His love is not like that of Adam's. God's love is a sacrificial love. He is also an understanding and forgiving God. So, instead of imposing and implementing the perpetual penalty for sin, He mitigated it Himself. It was God Himself who devised the remedy for man's sin, and that remedy is called "the plan of redemption."

What is that plan? God sent His Son incarnate in the flesh to do this job. His name is Jesus. He shed His blood and died on the cross to provide redemption for fallen man. He arose from the dead to give all of us the assurance of salvation (resurrection). If anyone may ask, how can I be saved? It is simple and free. Right now, repent of your sins, open your heart, invite Jesus to come in,and accept Him as your Lord and Savior. Get yourself a Bible and start reading from the New Testament. Find a Christian church where you can fellowship with God's people and grow spiritually. Then, you will have the assurance of the salvation by faith that Jesus paid for.

TEACHING 31

KNOWING CHRIST IS KNOWING GOD

If you had known Me, you would have known My Father also;
and from now on you know Him and have seen Him.

John 14:7

Of all of God's creation, man was His crown jewel, for he was special and unique. Why is this so? The rest of God's creation, animate or inanimate, had only one connection — with earth — whereas, man had two connections — with God and the earth. It was this connection with God that made man religious, even after he had fallen into sin.

Only man was created in the image and likeness of God. Only man had a direct and close contact with God. God was walking and talking with man. He gave man dominion over all His creation; man was God's vicar on earth.

In olden times, rulers put their own images on statues located around their domain and also on their money (coins). This was to remind their subjects of who ruled. But when man fell into sin, his connection to God was cut, and his fellowship with God was severed. As a result, man died spiritually, and slowly but surely, physical death began creeping in ... until eventually death conquered man, so that all men died.

This was not only a sad and sorry episode in the history of mankind, but also a tragic one. Adam lost nearly everything, especially the things of eternal value, which included the potential to become immortal. He constructively relinquished his dominion over God's creation to the devil, and this was an act of treason. He gained Eve all right and the pleasure of being with her, but only for a season. In the end, they both died, leaving a legacy of misery and the curse. After that terrible beginning, man wandered in darkness. Not only had the cataract of sin blurred his spiritual vision, but his decision to be independent from God had totally blinded him.

Despite the fallen nature of man, however, there was still a longing in him, because of his created connection, for God. There was a vacuum in his being that nothing or no one else could fill or satisfy except God. This led men to invent various religions, to fill this vacuum, but all of them were based on an ignorance of God. Man worshipped the creature instead of the Creator.

Although the evidence of God through nature has been overwhelming and undeniable, still men did not know God, or maybe they just chose to ignore Him. This is the reason there are so many religions in the world today.

Thank God for His grace and mercy. He did not want this ignorance of His person to continue, and therefore, He revealed Himself. First, He revealed Himself to individuals, and then He revealed Himself to an entire nation, the people of Israel.

Prior to the advent of the New Testament, the Hebrew people were the only ones who had knowledge of the true and right concepts of God. When Jesus came, the knowledge of God became available for all nations. Whereas in nature, the evidence of God was visualized, in Jesus, it was verbalized as the Word of God. Jesus Christ is *"the express image"* of the invisible God (Hebrews 13). This Word *express* means "to make known." It also means "to speak." So, if we want to know God, look at Jesus. He is God!

Look to Jesus. Believe His words, and believe His works. Acquaint yourself with Him now and be at peace, so that good will come upon you. Repent of your sins, receive Jesus Christ as your Lord and Savior, and you will be saved!

POOR BUT PROSPEROUS

Then He lifted up His eyes toward His disciples, and said:

"Blessed are you poor,
For yours is the kingdom of God."   Luke 6:20

How relevant is the Gospel of our Lord Jesus Christ to the poor today? One sister in the Lord answered with a question: "Who are the poor?"

I said, "Good question. Do you know?"

She did not answer.

A pastor answered and said, "Very relevant." I asked him to elaborate but he, likewise, did not answer.

During the early ministry of Jesus, many, if not most, of those who followed Him were poor people. They were the sick, the outcasts, the slaves and the children. Categorized, they were the spiritually poor, the physically poor, the materially and financially poor and also the socially and politically poor.

What were the indicators that these groups of people could be considered poor? First, they had been reduced to begging, and second, they were dependant upon the welfare of others.

That's why children are included, because they depend on their parents to sustain them. Without that support from their parents, many children would perish.

Poor people beg because their survival and existence depend on the generosity of their benefactors. Such was the case with Lazarus who begged at the rich man's table. Unfortunately, the rich man was unwilling to share with him, so Lazarus died (see Luke 16).

Actually, all people — whether poor or rich — are spiritually poor in the eyes of God, even though most of them don't realize their spiritual condition. When Jesus said, *"Blessed are the poor ... ,"* He was not inferring that spiritual, physical or economic poverty was a blessing. The blessedness of those poor was in begging for and depending on the grace and mercy of God.

True Christians have this kind of attitude from the time they are saved. This attitude continues because they are forever dependent upon God for spiritual sustenance. This is why Paul, even though he had already met Christ, wrote, *"That I may know him ..."* (Philippians 3:10).

The spiritually poor who beg and children have one thing in common: they are both heirs of the Kingdom of Heaven. Jesus said:

> *Assuredly, I say to you, unless you are converted and become as little children, you will by no means enter the kingdom of heaven.* Matthew 18:3

Today prosperity, as promised by God to the followers of Christ in the Bible, has become quite a controversial issue among pastors and preachers. This prosperity promise is comprehensive, covering spiritual and physical, as well as economic. God, through the pages of the Bible, says it this way:

POOR BUT PROSPEROUS

Beloved, I wish above all things that thou mayest prosper and be
in health, even as thy soul prospereth.   3 John 2, KJV

What a wonderful promise!

First, God calls us beloved, and then He says He wants us to prosper. I believe that, and I have experienced it. I was once a very poor pastor, but God has prospered me. Yes, we can be spiritually poor, as I have explained, and still be prosperous.

There are pastors and preachers who attribute the wonderful prosperity promise of God to the devil. To my way of thinking, they are themselves agents and advocates of the devil. Because they preach the bad news of unbelief, they have no business being pastors or preachers in the Church of the Lord Jesus Christ. Let them be part of the media, where they, no doubt, will continue to broadcast their bad news. You and I must believe the truth and prosper.

THE GOD OF BLESSINGS

And God blessed them, saying, "Be fruitful, and multiply, and fill the waters in the seas, and let birds multiply on the earth." Then God blessed them, and God said to them, "Be fruitful and multiply; fill the earth and subdue it; have dominion over the fish of the sea, over the birds of the air, and over every living thing that moves on the earth." Genesis 1:22 and 28, KJV

Our God is a God of blessing. This was one of His intentions when He created the world that we live in, including us human beings. In fact, the Bible shows that God pronounced these blessings twice. That's a double blessing.

Our God is also a God of order. He has established certain laws and principles, in keeping with His divine purpose, in order to set in motion and harmony His created system. Breaking these laws and principles would cause derailment and derangement of the order and harmony, not only of the relationship between God and man, but also the created earth itself. This was an offence against God. The other word we use is *sin*.

Sin has two sides to its coin — the sin of commission and the sin of omission. When a person is precluded by God from doing a certain thing, and he goes ahead and does it anyway, that's a sin of commission. When one is ordered by God to do something, and he fails to do it, that's a sin of omission.

The incident that occurred in the Garden of Eden, as described in Genesis 3, is not only a sad and sorry one, but also a tragedy. Instead of living a life with the blessings of God, Adam and Eve brought a curse upon themselves and the earth because of their disobedience to God's law. This curse has permeated the entire human race and caused untold misery, hardships, disaster, suffering, sickness, sorrow, pain and death.

The Old Testament ends with the word *curse* because that is the legacy man left. However, God's people, through His grace and mercy, can reverse the curse and regain His blessings. How? By obeying God's Word and His will.

Abraham was an example. God said to Abraham (formerly Abram):

"Get out of your country,
From your family
And from your father's house,
To a land that I will show you.
I will make you a great nation;
I will bless you
And make your name great;
And you shall be a blessing.
I will bless those who bless you,
And I will curse him who curses you;
And in you all the families of the earth shall be blessed."

Genesis 12:1-3

Another example was God's promise of blessing to the children of Israel after they had come out of Egypt. God said to them:

> Now it shall come to pass, if you diligently obey the voice of the LORD your God, to observe carefully all His commandments which I command you today, that the LORD your God will set you high above all nations of the earth. And all these blessings shall come upon you and overtake you, because you obey the voice of the LORD your God:
> Blessed shall you be in the city, and blessed shall you be in the country.
> Blessed shall be the fruit of your body, the produce of your ground and the increase of your herds, the increase of your cattle and the offspring of your flocks.
> Blessed shall be your basket and your kneading bowl.
> Blessed shall you be when you come in, and blessed shall you be when you go out.
> The LORD will cause your enemies who rise against you to be defeated before your face; they shall come out against you one way and flee before you seven ways.
> The LORD will command the blessing on you in your storehouses and in all to which you set your hand, and He will bless you in the land which the LORD your God is giving you.
>
> Deuteronomy 28:1-8

The birth of Jesus Christ in the New Testament was the highest of God's blessings. Jesus was to be a blessing to all mankind, not just for God's chosen nation or a select few people. He was to bring the blessing of salvation, if we believe in Him and accept Him as our Lord and Savior. This blessing far exceeds any earthly blessings, which are but temporal.

Now, through Jesus Christ, we can even gain heavenly blessings, and these will be good for all eternity. Hallelujah! Praise God!

Our Lord Jesus commenced His ministry by pronouncing blessings to the unblessed:

Blessed are the poor in spirit ... .   Matthew 5:3

Blessed are those who mourn ... .   Matthew 5:4

Blessed are the meek ... .   Matthew 5:5

Blessed are those who hunger and thirst for righteousness ... .
                    Matthew 5:6

Blessed are the merciful ... .   Matthew 5:7

Blessed are the pure in heart ... .   Matthew 5:8

Blessed are the peacemakers ... .   Matthew 5:9

Blessed are those who are persecuted for righteousness' sake
... .   Matthew 5:10

Blessed are you ... .   Matthew 5:11

God has blessed us *"with all spiritual blessings in heavenly places in Christ"* (Ephesians 1:3). So, Christians, let us obey the Lord and be faithful. Stop feeling self-pity and feeling poor

and miserable, and start praising and thanking God. Claim
and count your blessings now. His Word declares:

> *The blessing of the LORD makes one rich,*
> *And He adds no sorrow with it.*   Proverbs 10:22

Amen!

GOD WAS BETRAYED — TWICE

So He left them, went away again, and prayed the third time, saying the same words. Then He came to His disciples and said to them, "Are you still sleeping and resting? Behold, the hour is at hand, and the Son of Man is being betrayed into the hands of sinners. Rise, let us be going. See, My betrayer is at hand."

Matthew 26:44-46

History repeats itself. This is also true in the redemptive history of man, and it shows us that man has never really learned his lesson.

It is interesting to note that both of these horrendous acts of betrayal against God took place in a similar venue — a garden. The first one was in the Garden of Eden, and the second one was in the Garden of Gethsemane.

What was the reason for these double betrayals? Love. With the first, it was the love of a woman, and with the second it was the love of money (by Judas).

Betrayal is a serious crime, and it affects many. Other than self-defense, killing is permitted under our Philippine constitution in only one other instance. That is when a man catches his wife in the act of carnal knowledge with an illicit lover. Under our law, he is exonerated from penalty if he kills either or both of them. I am not suggesting that a Christian husband should do this, if the situation should ever arise. To me, this situation is one where divorce would be a justifiable option. Instead of killing your spouse, live and let live. Let the guilty party stand before the law and before God. That is justice enough.

So, let us be faithful to one another and faithful to God. Don't betray a spouse, and don't betray God. Why? The Scriptures answer this way:

> *It is a fearful thing to fall into the hands of the living God.*
>
> Hebrews 10:31

Amen!

DELUDED AND DECEIVED CHRISTIANS

Then the LORD God took the man and put him in the garden of Eden to tend and keep it. And the LORD God commanded the man, saying, "Of every tree of the garden you may freely eat; but of the tree of the knowledge of good and evil you shall not eat, for in the day that you eat of it you shall surely die."   Genesis 2:15-17

Many of mainstream Christians still believe and teach that man was immortal when God created him and remained that way until his fall. This is completely and absolutely contrary to what the Bible teaches. We believe, as Christians, that the Bible is the Word of God and is the final authority in matters of our Christian belief and life. The Bible is the paragon of truth. So let's look at what the Bible says regarding this issue of human mortality before man sinned against God.

The Garden of Eden was the home of Adam that God provided for him. It was filled with many trees. Some of those trees were ornamental, but others were for food. In the midst of the garden were two special trees: (1) The Tree of Life, and (2) The Tree of the Knowledge of Good and Evil.

God gave Adam two express mandates concerning these trees. The first was, *"Of every tree of the garden you may freely eat."* The second was, *"But of the tree of the knowledge of good and evil you shall not eat, for in the day that you eat of it you shall surely die."* This indicates that man was mortal.

Mortal means "subject to death." These two mandates formed the nature of a law. The first one was practical, and the second one was punitive. The second one was also a *mala prohibita.* [2]

Then, enter the devil, pretending to be a serpent. He says to the woman: *"Has God indeed said, 'You shall not eat of every tree of the garden'?"* (Genesis 3:1).

The woman answered, *"We may eat the fruit of the trees of the garden; but of the fruit of the tree which is in the midst of the garden, God has said, 'You shall not eat it, nor shall you touch it, lest you die' "* (Genesis 3:2-3).

The serpent disagreed: *"You will not surely die. For God knows that in the day you eat of it your eyes will be opened, and you will be like God, knowing good and evil"* (Genesis 3:4-5).

Who was telling the truth? Of course, God was telling the truth. And who was telling a lie? Of course, the devil was telling the lie.

Now, history is repeating itself. The devil is still in the business of deceiving, and he is deceiving pastors and preachers of mainstream Christianity. This is alarming. Pastors and preachers, wake up! Are you blind? Are you ignorant of the Scriptures? Are you without understanding? Abandon and discard this teaching now. Why? Because it is of the devil.

Will they hear? Probably not because, just like Eve, they are deluded and deceived!

---

2. *Mala prohibita* (singular malum prohibitum) is a term applied to any action that is criminalized strictly by statute and statutory law. The phrase is Latin, and translates as "wrong because it is prohibited."

DREADFUL, DESTRUCTIVE
AND DEADLY DEMONS

*The thief does not come except to steal, and to kill, and to destroy.
I have come that they may have life, and that they may have it
more abundantly.*   John 10:10

Through stealth, and disguised as a serpent, the chief of all demons, called the devil, lured Eve into a death trap, by enticing her to eat of the forbidden tree. His specialty is deceit, temptation, destruction and death. Jesus described him well in John 10:10. Far too often we are unaware that the cause of our misery, misfortunes and mishaps is the devil himself.

Where did demons come from? Demons are fallen angels. The Bible shows that the devil was once an archangel whose name was Lucifer. He was created perfect, but he later sinned. The particular sin found in him was pride (see Isaiah 14).

Lucifer, together with a third of all the angelic hosts of Heaven, rebelled against God. As a result, they were cast out of Heaven. Jesus confirmed this when He said, *"I saw Satan [another name for the devil, which means "enemy of God and man"]) fall like lightning from heaven"* (Luke 10:18).

There are two kinds of demons (as far as their status is concerned): (1) those demons that roam around free and (2) those demons that are incarcerated in the abyss. The name of the leader of the incarcerated demons is Abaddon, also known as Apollyon. These demons look hideous, grotesque, bizarre and terrifying. They will be unleashed in the apocalyptic future to wreck havoc upon the people of the earth. Their sting will torment people with excruciating pain, so much so that men will seek death, but death will elude them for five months. One third of the total population of the earth will eventually be killed by these demons from Hell (see Revelation 9).

During His earthly ministry, Jesus delivered many people who were possessed by demons. For instance, one day a demoniac who lived among the tombs came out to meet Him. Some had attempted to bind this man with chains, but he was so strong that he broke the chains. No one could control him. People were afraid to pass by the place where he lived because he was always shouting and cutting himself with stones. He recognized Jesus and, in fact, worshipped Him. He begged Jesus not to torment him before the time, but Jesus commanded the demons to come out of the man, and the man was instantly delivered. Afterward he was found sitting with Jesus, clothed and in his right mind (see Mark 5).

Mary Magdalene was among those whom Jesus delivered from the captivity and control of demons. She'd had seven demons. Can you imagine having seven demons? No wonder she loved Jesus so much that she followed Him, even to Calvary.

Mary Magdalene was still there when Jesus was resurrected. He said:

But if I cast out demons by the Spirit of God, surely the kingdom of God has come upon you.   Matthew 12:28

Therefore if the Son makes you free, you shall be free indeed.

John 8:36

Warning: If you have been delivered from demon possession and you are now clean and empty, don't remain empty for long. Otherwise, the demon who was ejected will come back to visit you, and if he finds you empty, he will invite more demons to join him in possessing you again, so that your situation will become much worse than before (see Matthew 12:43-45).

To fill yourself with God, find a good Bible-believing church and fellowship with God's people. Fill yourself with God's Word and His Spirit, and don't give the devil any place in your life. When he tempts you, resist him, and he will flee from you, in the name of Jesus!

Amen!

HOW THE MIGHTY BECAME MEEK

And Moses was learned in all the wisdom of the Egyptians, and
was mighty in words and deeds.   Acts 7:22

In spite of his royal upbringing, Moses, when he was grown, began to identify with His Israelite people. One day when he visited them he saw one of them being mistreated by an Egyptian. Going to the man's defense, Moses killed the Egyptian. He thought that surely his people would realize that God wanted to use him to rescue them from their terrible slavery, but they did not.

The next day Moses came upon two Israelites who were fighting. He tried to reconcile them by saying, "Men, you are brothers. Why do you want to hurt each other?" But the man who was mistreating the other pushed Moses aside and said, "Who made you ruler and judge over us? Do you want to kill me, as you killed the Egyptian yesterday?" (see Exodus 2:14). When Pharaoh, the king of Egypt, heard about this, he tried to kill Moses, and Moses was forced to flee to Midian, where he remained for the next forty years.

In Midian, Moses married Zipporah, one of the daughters of Jethro, the priest of Midian. Zipporah bore Moses a son, and he was named Gershom, which meant, *"I have been a stranger in a foreign land"* (Exodus 2:22).

During that long period, Moses worked as a shepherd, tending the flocks of his father-in law near Mount Horeb, the mountain of God. Then one day, the Angel of the Lord appeared there on that mountain in flames of fire coming from within a bush. When Moses went up to see this extraordinary phenomenon, he was amazed to see that the bush appeared to be on fire, but it did not burn up. What could this mean?

As Moses approached the burning bush, God called to him from within the bush, *"Moses, Moses!"* (Exodus 3:4).

Moses answered, *"Here I am"* (verse 4).

"Do not draw near this place," God said. *"Take your sandals off your feet, for the place where you stand is holy ground"* (verse 5). Moses was in the presence of God, and God was talking to him.

God continued: *"I am the God of your father—the God of Abraham, the God of Isaac, and the God of Jacob"* (verse 6).

For his part, Moses hid his face because he was afraid to look at God.

It was God's turn again:

And the Lord said: "I have surely seen the oppression of My people who are in Egypt, and have heard their cry because of their taskmasters, for I know their sorrows. So I have come down to deliver them out of the hand of the Egyptians, and to bring them up from that land to a good and large land, to a land flowing with milk and honey, to the place of the Canaanites and the Hittites and the Amorites and the Perizzites and the Hivites and the Jebusites. Now therefore, behold, the cry of the children of Israel has come to Me, and I have also seen the oppression with which the Egyptians oppress them. Come now, therefore, and I will send

*you to Pharaoh that you may bring My people, the children of
Israel, out of Egypt."* Exodus 3:7-10

Moses objected: *"Who am I that I should go to Pharaoh, and that I
should bring the children of Israel out of Egypt?"* (verse 11).

God's answer was: *"I will certainly be with you"* (verse 12).

Between Moses' life in Egypt and his life in Midian, forty more
years had now gone by. That made him eighty years old when
he talked with God on Mt. Horeb. While most ministers of the
Gospel today retire at sixty-five, Moses was just getting starting
at eighty. Hallelujah!

What happened to Moses during those forty years in Midian? He did the seemingly mundane task of shepherding his
father-in-law's flocks. What must have gone through his mind
during those forty years? Did he regret his decision to renounce
his Egyptian privileges? What was his feeling toward his fellow
Israelites in Egypt? Had he lost faith and hope in God? Was he
now a total failure, as far as the mission of delivering his people
from Egyptian slavery and oppression was concerned? These
are interesting and intriguing questions, and the Bible does not
reveal most of the answers. We can only imagine. Only God and
Moses know for sure.

But perhaps you and I, if we try to put ourselves in Moses' shoes
(or sandals, in his case), can answer some of these questions. What
would be the answer based on our personal experiences? If you
ask me, I would say, "Of course, it would have been a normal and
expected reaction to feel like a failure and to lose faith and hope
after so many years of waiting. I, personally, would have been
deeply disappointed and hurt that, after all the sacrifices I had
made and my well-intentioned motives to help my people, I had
become disgraced and rejected. It was an extreme degradation.

234

Quite honestly, I don't know what I would have done or how I would have reacted. It is a difficult question for us to answer, as we are only spectators in this narrative of Moses' ordeal. Would we feel like a total failure? Would we feel self-pity? Oh, yes, I think so.

And yet, through it all, the faith of Moses developed and became a living reality. In Egypt, he had endured as seeing the invisible God through the eyes of faith (probably by means of his mother's teachings). Now, at Mount Horeb, Moses was able to actually see God face-to-face. So he clearly had no problem with his relationship with God.

Moses' troubles were with himself, with the people of God and with Pharaoh, King of Egypt. These brought him disappointment and failure. But Moses overcame all of these troubles through a change of attitude. In Egypt, he was mighty, but with God at Mount Horeb, he became meek. What changed Moses? Was it his troubles? Or was it his forty years in Midian? I believe that it was seeing God face-to-face and being in His presence. If we want to succeed in our service to God, we must not only rely on our own thoughts or what other people think, but we must totally depend on and rely on God. We must never use God, but, instead, allow Him to use us.

Amen!

TEACHING 38

NONE OF THESE DISEASES

If you diligently heed the voice of the LORD your God and do what is right in His sight, give ear to His commandments and keep all His statutes, I will put none of the diseases on you which I have brought on the Egyptians. For I am the LORD who heals you.

Exodus 15:26

Following the crossing of the Red Sea by the Israelites, Moses led them through the Desert of Shur. They traveled for three days without finding water, and when they came to a place called Marah, they could not drink the water there because it was bitter. The people grumbled against Moses, so he cried out to the Lord, and the Lord showed him a piece of wood. He threw that piece of wood into the water, and the water became sweet. It was there that God gave His people the promise: NONE OF THESE DISEASES.

This was the first decree or law given to the Israelites by God after they came out of Egypt. The object of the law, healing and freedom from disease, was incumbent upon their obedience to God's Word. This was a quasi-contract, and the two parties involved were God and the Israelite people. The stipulated conditions of the contract were as follows: for the Israelites, they had to listen,

NONE OF THESE DISEASES

do what was right in God's sight, obey and keep His commands. The obligation of God was not to put any of these diseases upon them but, instead, to be their Healer.

First of all, let us ask this question: do all diseases come from God? The answer is no, not all diseases come from God. It is obvious in this case, however, that it was God who put certain diseases upon the Egyptians. Those diseases were some sort of punishment for the fact that the Egyptians had defied God's commands. Disobeying God's commands brings consequences and has a punitive effect. Allowing the Egyptians to suffer sickness was divine justice, and that is God's sovereign prerogative.

More often than not, disease comes from the devil. The case of Job is a good example:

> *So Satan [another name for the devil] went out from the presence of the LORD and afflicted Job with painful sores from the soles of his feet to the crown of his head.* Job 2:7

The devil always has bad intentions, and his motives for inflicting diseases on people are based on envy, his whims, pure caprice and his delight in doing evil. As Jesus said, " *The thief does not come except to steal, and to kill, and to destroy"* (John 10:10).

So, why did God say that He would heal His people and, at the same time promise *"none of these diseases"*? This principle of divine healing does not apply in the first instance. It applies to the second and the third instances, when the diseases comes from the devil and when God's people are vulnerable to disease by reason of their careless or promiscuous living. The sins of the past can bring diseases, even though we have already repented of those sins.

Who do you think healed Job of his diseases inflicted by the devil? Of course, it was God who healed him. So, in these last two instances, God is the Healer of His people.

Being human, however, makes us vulnerable to sickness and disease, so sometimes we can't blame either God or the devil for our diseases. Careless and promiscuous living and a disregard for proper hygiene can bring on self-invited sicknesses. The old saying, "Cleanliness is next to godliness" is true.

Not too long ago, the major health concern in the world was AIDS. Now, at this writing, it is the Ebola virus. This deadly disease has killed more than six thousand in three West African countries in recent years, and cases have diagnosed in several other countries. Nations are terrified of this disease reaching their borders.

But the Ebola outbreak is nothing compared with the great wave of Bubonic Plague, also known as the Black Death, that reached pandemic proportions during the Middle Ages. The disease swept China, Europe and India and killed more than one hundred million people. It was the biggest killer of all times. What was the Black Death? It was an infection thought to be carried by the fleas on rats. These rats boarded ships and were carried all over the world, thus spreading the infection far and wide.

One of the ministry strategies of our Lord Jesus Christ during His evangelistic outreaches was healing the people's diseases:

Then Jesus went about all the cities and villages, teaching in their synagogues, preaching the gospel of the kingdom, and healing every sickness and every disease among the people. Matthew 9:35

The people brought to Him all who were ill with various diseases, those suffering severe pain, the demon-possessed, those having seizures, and the paralyzed, and He healed them all. In this way, Jesus practically wiped out sickness and disease in the Palestine of His day. His earthly ministry envisioned a time when there would be: *"none of these diseases."*

The subject of divine healing relative to human diseases is very relevant and material in our contemporary Christian life. God has promised divine healing then and now, since the time of Moses and the Israelites until today:

Jesus Christ is the same yesterday, today, and forever.
Hebrews 13:8

He honors those who fear the LORD;
He who swears to his own hurt and does not change.
Psalm 15:4

Several of God's promises regarding divine healing are:

I am the LORD [Jehovah Rapha] who heals you.   Exodus 15:26

Who Himself bore our sins in His own body on the tree, that we, having died to sins, might live for righteousness— by whose stripes you were healed.   1 Peter 2:24

For with God nothing will be impossible.   Luke 1:37

I believe in divine healing. Our eldest son had epilepsy when he was a little boy. My wife and I prayed for his healing, and God healed him. That was the last seizure he ever had.

My wife had a stroke a couple of years ago. Her face was dis-figured, and she could hardly move her arm. She prayed to God by herself, invoking His promise of divine healing, and she was healed. Now, her face looks beautiful again, and she can move her arm normally.

Glory to God! Hallelujah! Have faith in God!

Prayer, the Most Important Conversation of Man

In this manner, therefore, pray ... .   Matthew 6:9

Why is prayer the most important conversation a man can ever have? Because he is talking with God Almighty. Therefore he must be discreet with his words and consider the form and substance of his prayer. There are prayers which are full of nonsense and redundancy, and Jesus has precluded Christians from uttering such prayers.

What dos it mean to pray from the heart? It means to pray with intelligence. In other words, think before you pray, and don't pray haphazardly. Jesus taught us how to pray and so what He taught us is important.

A rabbi once told his son: "Son, always remember this, and don't ever forget it. Be honest and never ever tell a lie. But you also don't have to tell the whole truth." And he was right. We would have so many less problems in our world today if people would just stop lying, cheating and stealing. Be honest with God.

Don't shout at God when you pray. Why? Because God is not deaf. It is disrespectful to shout at Him. Those who pray to God must lower their voices and approach Him in fear and trembling. After all, a mere man is talking with His Royal Majesty, the King of Kings and Lord of Lords!

It is all right to shout at the devil and his demons, especially when rebuking them and casting them away.

We must open our mouths and utter the words when we pray. Prayer is the expression of our hearts to God. Some perhaps don't know how to pray or are embarrassed to pray in public, especially in restaurants. Never be ashamed of God, and He will never be ashamed of you.

Amen!

A PRELUDE TO CHRISTMAS

There was in the days of Herod, the king of Judea, a certain priest named Zacharias, of the division of Abijah. His wife was of the daughters of Aaron, and her name was Elizabeth. And they were both righteous before God, walking in all the commandments and ordinances of the Lord blameless. But they had no child, because Elizabeth was barren, and they were both well advanced in years. So it was, that while he was serving as priest before God in the order of his division, according to the custom of the priesthood, his lot fell to burn incense when he went into the temple of the Lord. And the whole multitude of the people was praying outside at the hour of incense. Then an angel of the Lord appeared to him, standing on the right side of the altar of incense. And when Zacharias saw him, he was troubled, and fear fell upon him.
But the angel said to him, "Do not be afraid, Zacharias, for your prayer is heard; and your wife Elizabeth will bear you a son, and you shall call his name John." Luke 1:5-13

Whereas the Old Testament ends with the word *curse*, the New Testament commences with blessings, double blessings as a matter of fact. These blessings were foretold in an announcement by no ordinary herald, but by the angel Gabriel who stands in the presence of God. Gabriel was sent to godly and devout people to inform them of the extraordinary births of two infants. The first announcement concerned the birth of John the Baptist and the second the birth of Jesus Himself. John the Baptist was to be the forerunner of our Lord Jesus Christ, and to pave the way for His earthly ministry.

The first appearance of Gabriel was to Zacharias in the Temple in Jerusalem. When Zacharias saw the angel, standing at the right side of the altar of incense, he was startled and even gripped with fear. The angel told him not to be afraid. His prayer had been heard. His wife Elizabeth would bear a son. He was to name him John.

The angel went on:

And you will have joy and gladness, and many will rejoice at his birth. For he will be great in the sight of the Lord, and shall drink neither wine nor strong drink. He will also be filled with the Holy Spirit, even from his mother's womb. And he will turn many of the children of Israel to the Lord their God. He will also go before Him in the spirit and power of Elijah, "to turn the hearts of the fathers to the children," and the disobedient to the wisdom of the just, to make ready a people prepared for the Lord.

Luke 1:14-17

Zacharias and Elizabeth had no children because she was barren. Added to this was the fact that they were both growing old. Both of these individuals were descendants of the priestly line, and the Bible says that they were upright in the sight of God, observing all the commandments and regulations blamelessly.

Zacharias doubted the words of the angel Gabriel that day regarding the good news of the birth of a son in his old age, and as a result, he was struck dumb, meaning that he could no longer speak. This continued to be his condition until the birth of his son John. When he completed his temple service that day and went home, Zacharias could only express himself through motions.

Nevertheless, a miracle happened. Elizabeth was soon pregnant, and she remained in seclusion for the next five months. She was a happy woman. She declared:

> *The Lord has done this for me. In these days he has shown his favor and taken away my disgrace among the people.*
>
> Luke 1:25, NIV

Then, in Elizabeth's sixth month, God sent the angel Gabriel on another similar assignment. This time he went to Nazareth, a small town in Galilee, to visit a virgin named Mary:

> *The angel went to her and said, "Greetings, you who are highly favored! The Lord is with you."*
> *Mary was greatly troubled at his words and wondered what kind of greeting this might be. But the angel said to her, "Do not be afraid, Mary; you have found favor with God. You will conceive and give birth to a son, and you are to call him Jesus. He will be great and will be called the Son of the Most High. The Lord God will give him the throne of his father David, and he will reign over Jacob's descendants forever; his kingdom will never end."*
> *"How will this be," Mary asked the angel, "since I am a virgin?"*
> *The angel answered, "The Holy Spirit will come on you, and the power of the Most High will overshadow you. So the holy one to*

be born will be called the Son of God. Even Elizabeth your rela-
tive is going to have a child in her old age, and she who was said
to be unable to conceive is in her sixth month. For no word from
God will ever fail."

"I am the Lord's servant," Mary answered. "May your word to
me be fulfilled." Then the angel left her. Luke 1:28-38, NIV

These two remarkable and extraordinary events leading up to the birth of Jesus were characterized by the miraculous. Zacharias and Elizabeth were beyond childbearing age, and Elizabeth was barren. They must have been praying for a child because the angel said to them, *"Your prayer has been heard."* The answer to their prayer was a miracle baby, John the Baptist.

Mary was a virgin, and it would take a miracle for her to become impregnated. Through divine intervention, she also received a miracle baby, Jesus. All of these miracles were covered in one statement by the angel Gabriel:

For with God nothing will be impossible. Luke 1:37

Is this message still relevant and material to us as Christians even in our contemporary times? Does God still do miracles? Does God still answer prayer? These are good questions, and they are relevant and material. I don't know about you, but I believe that God still does miracles today, and He still answers prayer. Maybe we're not having miracle babies these days, as did Elizabeth and Mary, but we have many other miraculous blessings.

Maybe the miracle you need is money. As the managing director of a mission and school, I have an enormous responsibility, especially in the area of finances. Our school, with more than two thousand children enrolled in both the elementary and high school, is a non-profit educational institution. Many of those children are not able to pay because they are from very poor families. We have more than ninety teachers and employees who expect their regular salaries and benefits twice each month.

My biggest financial burden comes each December. During that month, we are mandated by law to provide an extra month's pay for all of our teachers and workers. That alone requires ₱1 million. I can say that in twenty-five years of operation of our Star of Hope in the Philippines, God has never failed us. He has always provided that extra ₱1 million every December. Praise the Lord! And glory to God! He has angels from many places who send in the money just in time. Hallelujah! So we always have a blessed and merry Christmas.

REMEMBER LOT'S WIFE!

Remember Lot's wife.   Luke 17:32

One of the shortest verses in the Bible, these words were uttered by our Lord Jesus Christ, and they have serious warning implications still today.

The context of this passage speaks of two unprecedented cataclysmic events in the history of mankind. The first catastrophe was the universal deluge during the time of Noah, when all flesh perished (including every man who was not on the ark), in a watery grave. Only eight people survived the flood, together with the various animals in the ark.

The second catastrophe referred to here was the destruction of Sodom and Gomorrah with the other cities of the plain. All the inhabitants of those cities were incinerated with fire and brimstone, and only three souls escaped. These were God's early judgments on sinful mankind and a grim reality indeed.

When Jesus expounded these two terrifying Old Testament events, He was validating them as historical facts, and He was saying that the same type of devastating destruction will reoccur during the *"day of the Lord,"* which will transpire in the end times.

A repetition of a worldwide catastrophic flood has been already ruled out. In his covenant with Noah, God promised that He would never again destroy all of mankind by means of a universal flood. There is a probability, however, that the next divine judgment to be visited upon mankind will come by fire, as hinted at by Jesus when He cited the tragic incident at Sodom and Gomorrah.

Now who was Lot's wife? And, for that matter, who was Lot? The book of Genesis tells us that Lot was Abraham's nephew, who joined him when God called Abraham to go to Canaan. In time, Lot and his Uncle Abraham had a disagreement because of a skirmish between their respective herdsmen, and Abraham suggested that they part ways in order to avoid further misunderstanding. Abraham remained in Canaan, while Lot settled in Sodom.

With regards to Lot's wife, there is no indication in the book of Genesis that she was from the same country as Lot, so there is a strong probability that she was actually from Sodom itself. Sodom was a prosperous place at the time, but the men of Sodom were said to be *"exceedingly wicked and sinful against the LORD"* (Genesis 13:13).

Two angels, appearing as humans, came to Sodom and Gomorrah in order to execute God's judgment upon those places because of the gross sinfulness and sexual perversion (sodomy) of their citizens. Lot, his wife and two daughters were commanded to get out with haste from the city and escape for their lives because the time had come that the Lord would destroy those cities. The angels emphatically warned then not to look back:

> *Escape for your life! Do not look behind you nor stay anywhere in the plain. Escape to the mountains, lest you be destroyed.*
>
> Genesis 19:17

When Lot, his wife and his daughters were out of Sodom and on their way to a designated place of refuge, the Lord rained down fire and brimstone from Heaven and destroyed those cities with their inhabitants. Lot's wife could not help herself. She looked back:

> *But his wife looked back behind him, and she became a pillar of salt.* Genesis 19:26

She was out of Sodom, but Sodom was not yet out of her. Jesus said:

> *You are the salt of the earth; but if the salt loses its flavor, how shall it be seasoned? It is then good for nothing but to be thrown out and trampled underfoot by men.* Matthew 5:13

Don't look back to your sin and your old sinful life, but rather, look to Jesus, the Author and Finisher of our faith. He invites you now to come to Him. Receive Him as your Lord and Savior, and you will be saved. He said:

> *Come to Me, all you who labor and are heavy laden, and I will give you rest. Take My yoke upon you and learn from Me, for I am gentle and lowly in heart, and you will find rest for your souls.* Matthew 11:28-29

THE AGGRAVATING CIRCUMSTANCES OF SIN

For the wages of sin is death, but the gift of God is eternal life in Christ Jesus our Lord.   Romans 6:23

There are several judicial aspects that are analogous to sin, which was the consequence of Adam's disobedience. In political law, the violation of Adam and Eve was tantamount to treason. In civil law, it was an offense. The closest thing we can compare the sin of Adam and Eve to in criminal law is a crime. The apostle Paul did substantial explanation and elaboration in his writings regarding this judicial aspect, especially in the book of Romans. I presume that Paul was a lawyer before he was converted to Christ because he used legal terminology to explain our spiritual status before and after we accept Christ as our personal Lord and Savior.

The sin of Adam and Eve was a criminal act. It was a *mala prohibita*, in contradistinction to a *mala en se*, which act, by nature, is evil. An example of this crime is murder. Although there is nothing inherently evil in eating, it became evil when God precluded Adam and Eve from eating the fruit of the forbidden tree. God's command to them was this:

But of the tree of the knowledge of good and evil you shall not eat, for in the day that you eat of it you shall surely die.

Genesis 2:17

This included a punitive effect, meaning to say that Adam and Eve would be punished if they disobeyed God. What was their punishment? It was death, spiritual death. So it was capital punishment.

The punishment of Adam and Eve was clearly not physical death, as many Christians believe — including some pastors and theologians. How do we know this? By nature, they were already mortal, so even if they had not sinned, they would have died eventually. So there is a distinction between their nature and their act. Proof of this is that when Adam and Eve ate of the fruit anyway, they did not die (at least physically). They died spiritually.

Sin did not kill Adam and Eve physically, and conversely, when a person has Christ in him, that does not yet make him immortal. He will still die, awaiting resurrection to attain immortality.

The penalty for sin was fixed. It was spiritual death, the maximum penalty. Spiritual death implies separation from God, which is worse than physical death.

In criminal law, the circumstances surrounding the act of the crime may add burden to or make the penalty more severe. Spiritual death is what is called an accessory penalty, and it carries what is known as aggravating circumstances.

There are several elements to consider in order to determine that a crime committed carries with it a penalty that includes aggravating circumstances. Only one of these elements is required for an additional penalty to be imposed. So, what was the aggravating circumstance in the case of the sin of Adam and Eve? Their sin (the crime committed) was an insult, in contempt of and disregard for the respect due to the Sovereign Authority, none other than God Himself! And how was this accessory penalty imposed? It was imposed on the physical life of Adam and Eve, as well as upon all mankind through them.

To the woman, God said:

> *I will greatly multiply your sorrow and your conception;*
> *In pain you shall bring forth children;*
> *Your desire shall be for your husband,*
> *And he shall rule over you.*　　　　　　　　Genesis 3:16

To Adam, God said:

> *Cursed is the ground for your sake;*
> *In toil you shall eat of it*
> *All the days of your life.*
> *Both thorns and thistles it shall bring forth for you,*
> *And you shall eat the herb of the field.*
> *In the sweat of your face you shall eat bread*
> *Till you return to the ground,*
> *For out of it you were taken;*
> *For dust you are,*
> *And to dust you shall return.*　　　　　Genesis 3:17-19

What is the opposite of aggravating circumstances? It is mitigating circumstances. In the case of mitigating circumstances, the penalty imposed is alleviated or made less severe. Was there an element of mitigating circumstance in the crime of Adam and Eve? I see at least one element, and it is that their crime, or sin, was instigated by an outside force, and he seemed to them to be irresistible.

How were the mitigating circumstance implemented? They were implemented by implication, when the Lord God made garments of skin for Adam and Eve and clothed them Himself. Later, in the New Testament, our Lord Jesus Christ expressed that mitigating circumstance, when He said:

> *Come to Me, all you who labor and are heavy laden, and I will give you rest. Take My yoke upon you and learn from Me, for I am gentle and lowly in heart, and you will find rest for your souls. For My yoke is easy and My burden is light.*
>
> Matthew 11:28-30

This is good news indeed!

Since I responded to the call of Jesus through the Gospel, came to Him and accepted Him as my Lord and Savior, my life has been changed for the better. I no longer have to struggle with the burden of living in sin and the guilt of it because God has already forgiven me and He has provided all my needs.

As the pastor of a church, I don't receive much salary, but I have never complained about it. Somehow God always compensates me, not only in terms of having money and material things, but also in having good health and a loving and supportive wife and family. God has also given us favor with people who trusted us with ministry. We have sufficiency in Christ and more than enough, so that we are able to share with others and help the needy. Therefore, I am not a pauper pastor; I am living a mitigated Christian life.

Modesty aside, I have noticed that others who earn more money seem to always be in need. I have never understood why, in spite of their sizable income, they are in debt and are always borrowing money. Besides this, they are also miserable. Someone suggested that this might be due to a curse on them. If that is the case, their curse can be reversed and become a blessing. How? Right now, open your heart to God. Repent of your sins. Invite Jesus Christ into your heart and accept Him as your personal Lord and Savior. If you do this, your life will be changed into a blessed one.

God is a God of blessings. Even though you don't have much in terms of money or material possessions, as the saying goes: *"Little is much when God is in it."* The Scriptures teach:

> *The blessing of the LORD makes one rich,*
> *And He adds no sorrow with it.*　　　　Proverbs 10:22

The most wonderful news of all is that there exist justifying circumstances. This means that we will not incur criminal liability. We are absolved from the punishment of spiritual death and Hell. We will no longer be separated from God. Instead, we are reconciled to Him. Wow! How did that happen? Was there any element of justifying circumstance in the sinful (criminal) act of Adam and Eve to warrant this? No, there was none.

What then? Justifying circumstances are available to us through a judicial act of the sovereign God. He provided it through the sacrificial death of His Son, Jesus Christ, on the cross of Calvary. We call this act grace and mercy. This is what Paul was talking all about in the book of Romans. Among other things, he wrote:

> *Therefore, having been justified by faith, we have peace with God*
> *through our Lord Jesus Christ, through whom also we have access*
> *by faith into this grace in which we stand, and rejoice in hope of*
> *the glory of God.*　　　　Romans 5:1-2

There is therefore now no condemnation to those who are in Christ Jesus, who do not walk according to the flesh, but according to the Spirit.
Romans 8:1

Therefore if the Son makes you free, you shall be free indeed.
Romans 8:36

Amen!

THE ESSENTIAL RIGHTEOUSNESS

For I say to you, that unless your righteousness exceeds the righteousness of the scribes and Pharisees, you will by no means enter the kingdom of heaven. Matthew 5:20

There are two kinds of righteousness that Jesus was talking about here. The first was the righteousness of the Pharisees and teachers of the Law. The second was a greater righteousness, and this second type of righteousness is the key to entering the Kingdom of Heaven.

This is the heart of the Sermon on the Mount, and this second righteousness is a condition precedent that must be in place before anyone can enter God's Kingdom. What is this second righteousness? It is the righteousness of God imputed, or credited, to man as a consequence of his faith in God and in His Son Jesus Christ.

The first righteousness is ruled out, as far as justification is concerned, because it is the righteousness of man, which, in the standard of God, is *"like filthy rags"* in His sight:

But we are all like an unclean thing,
And all our righteousnesses are like filthy rags;

We all fade as a leaf,
And our iniquities, like the wind,
Have taken us away.   Isaiah 64:6

What is righteousness? It is holy and upright living in accordance with God's standard. It is a moral concept, which literally means "straightness." Righteousness is the consequence of obedience to the laws of God.

In the Old Testament, the term *righteousness* was used to define man's relationship with God and with others. Although the Pharisees and the teachers of the Law were the most devout and pious of all men, when it came to the observance of the law, they fell short because they did not satisfy God's demand for righteousness. Paul confirmed this when he said:

There is none righteous, no, not one;
There is none who understands;
There is none who seeks after God.
They have all turned aside;
They have together become unprofitable;
There is none who does good, no, not one.   Romans 3:10-12

Paul meant that no one was able to fulfil the laws of God. Man could not be righteous in the sight of God on his own merits.

Is man hopeless then, with regards to obtaining the righteousness needed to enter the Kingdom of Heaven? The answer is no. Abraham, in the Old Testament, is a good example of how to obtain this acceptable righteousness. He was the forerunner of all believers.

In the book of Romans, Paul presented an extensive commentary on Abraham obtaining this acceptable righteousness. There he said that Abraham had believed God, and that his faith had been credited to him as righteousness:

> *He did not waver at the promise of God through unbelief, but was strengthened in faith, giving glory to God, and being fully convinced that what He had promised He was also able to perform. And therefore "it was accounted to him for righteousness."*
> *Now it was not written for his sake alone that it was imputed to him, but also for us. It shall be imputed to us who believe in Him who raised up Jesus our Lord from the dead, who was delivered up because of our offenses, and was raised because of our justification.*
> Romans 4:20-25

Nowadays, in New Testament times, the only way a man or woman can obtain the acceptable righteousness is through faith in Jesus Christ. He is the righteousness from God revealed to us. He is our righteousness.

In His Sermon on the Mount, Jesus said that He had come to fulfil the Law, something no one else could do. Therefore, when we believe in Jesus Christ, it is as if we had already fulfilled the Law in and through Him.

For this reason, it is always indispensable for us, in our evangelistic challenges to others to be saved, to make it clear to them that every person must receive Jesus Christ as personal Lord and Savior after repenting of their sins. It is in this way, one receives the righteousness of God in his life, which righteousness is the only way one can become acceptable to God.

When we accept Christ and His righteousness, God then sees us as righteous because of our identification, by faith, with His Son Jesus Christ. This gift of righteousness becomes the door that will open for anyone who is willing to enter the Kingdom of Heaven. Jesus also told His followers:

Blessed are those who hunger and thirst for righteousness,
    For they shall be filled.   Matthew 5:6

Amen!

THE GREATEST ESCAPE

Speak to the children of Israel, that they turn and camp before Pi Hahiroth, between Migdol and the sea, opposite Baal Zephon; you shall camp before it by the sea.

So the Egyptians pursued them, all the horses and chariots of Pharaoh, his horsemen and his army, and overtook them camping by the sea beside Pi Hahiroth, before Baal Zephon.

Exodus 14:2 and 9

After Moses and the Israelites had come out of Egypt, the Lord told them to camp by the sea. But when the King of Egypt was told that his Hebrew slaves had fled, he and his other officials changed their minds about releasing them. So he had his chariots made ready and took an army with six hundred of his best chariots along to pursue the Israelites. Thus Pharaoh, with all of his horses and chariots, went after the Israelites and soon overtook them as they camped by the sea.

As Pharaoh approached, the Israelites looked up, and there were the Egyptians, marching after them. They were terrified and cried out to the Lord. They said to Moses:

261

Because there were no graves in Egypt, have you taken us away to die in the wilderness? Why have you so dealt with us, to bring us up out of Egypt? Is this not the word that we told you in Egypt, saying, "Let us alone that we may serve the Egyptians"? For it would have been better for us to serve the Egyptians than that we should die in the wilderness.   Exodus 14:11-12

Moses answered them:

Do not be afraid. Stand still, and see the salvation of the LORD, which He will accomplish for you today. For the Egyptians whom you see today, you shall see again no more forever. The LORD will fight for you, and you shall hold your peace.

         Exodus 14:13-14

Then the Lord spoke to Moses:

Why do you cry to Me? Tell the children of Israel to go forward. But lift up your rod, and stretch out your hand over the sea and divide it. And the children of Israel shall go on dry ground through the midst of the sea.   Exodus 14:

Moses stretched out his hand over the sea, and all that night the Lord drove the waters back with a strong east wind, until the bottom of the sea had turned into dry land. The waters were divided, and the Israelites went through the sea on dry ground, with a wall of water on their right and another on their left. Undaunted, the Egyptians pursued, and all of Pharaoh's horses and chariots and horsemen followed into the sea.

Then the Lord spoke to Moses again to stretch out his hand over the sea so that the waters would flow back over the Egyptians and their chariots and horsemen. Moses did this, and at daybreak the sea flowed back into its place.

As the water flowed back, it covered the chariots and horsemen — the entire army of Pharaoh that had followed the Israelites into the sea. Not one Egyptian soldier survived that day. In this way, the Lord saved the Israelites from the hands of the Egyptians. When the Israelites saw the great power the Lord displayed against the Egyptians, they feared the Lord and put their trust in Him and in Moses His servant (see verse 31).

The exodus of the Israelites from Egypt was one of the most amazing, extraordinary, dramatic and fantastic events in the history of mankind. More than six hundred thousand men, besides women and children, were involved in this mass departure. They also brought along with them their livestock and their other belongings. The sheer number of people to guide and the volume of property to transport must have been a logistical nightmare for Moses, Aaron and the other elders. It was an immense task and responsibility for the leaders to bring these people through the desert and on to the Promise Land, said to be *"flowing with milk and honey"* (Exodus 3:8).

How did the Israelites know which way to go to reach their destination? They had no compasses yet. Did Moses or any of the other leaders know the way? The Bible shows that the Lord Himself was their Guide. By day He went ahead of them in a pillar of cloud, to guide them on their way, and by night He appeared to them in a pillar of fire to give them light and warmth. So the Israelites were able to travel by day and also by night. In all their journeying, neither the pillar of cloud by day nor the pillar of fire by night left its place before them.

Why did Pharaoh and his officials change their minds and pursue the Israelites into the desert? Was their motive to avenge the deaths of all the Egyptian firstborn? Were they bent on killing all the Israelites? No, Pharaoh and the Egyptians needed the Israelites alive, and the Israelites would have been no use to them dead. Life would now be very hard for the Egyptians without the accustomed services of their Israelite slaves. So, they wanted them alive, and they wanted to bring them back to Egypt.

Unfortunately for the Israelites, they actually felt they would rather go back to Egypt and continue serving the Egyptians, even under these cruel circumstances, rather than die in the desert. God knew this from the beginning. Rather than face their enemy, they would prefer to go back to Egypt and become slaves again. The Israelites were out of Egypt, but Egypt was not out of them yet. All they were thinking about was dying rather than depending on the Lord.

Did God want the Israelites to go back to Egypt? Absolutely not! Although there was a shorter route to the Promised Land, God led them through the desert, which was definitely a longer route. The reason was: if they had taken a shorter route, they might have encountered warlike inhabitants, and they might have changed their minds and gone back to Egypt.

God did not want His people to return to Egypt and be enslaved again by their former taskmasters. In fact, I believe that God helped the Israelites cross the Red Sea as on a dry ground, to keep them from turning back. Once the Israelites were on the other side of the sea, there was no way they could have returned to Egypt. They now had no other recourse than to proceed to the Promised Land, just as God had planned. This was God's purpose for the greatest escape ever, that His people would not return to Egypt.

Our Christian life is analogous to the life of the Israelites. It has been said that Christians are the spiritual Israelites. The journey of the Israelites to the Promised Land is similar in many aspects to our spiritual experiences, which are filled with many difficult challenges and testings. Christians are besieged with temptations, which are often recurring. We are surrounded with pressures from multiple perils, some of which are trials involving our physical health, finances, work and even relationships. Sometimes we are confused by all of this, and we don't know what to do. The Bible says that these temptations and trials are common to all followers of Christ (see 1 Corinthians 10:13). What is most reassuring in our journey of faith is this: just as the Lord was with the Israelites in their journey to the Promised Land, He is also with us — always. His providence and power will help us escape or overcome all obstacles and will give us victory in the name of Jesus Christ our Lord! Praise the Lord! Glory to His name! Hallelujah!

THE OTHER TREE

The LORD God made all kinds of trees grow out of the ground —
trees that were pleasing to the eye and good for food. In the middle
of the garden were the tree of life and the tree of the knowledge of
good and evil.   Genesis 2:9

After God created Adam and Eve, He put them in the Garden
of Eden. That garden was filled with various kinds of trees. Some
of these trees were ornamental, while several were for food, and
others were both ornamental and practical. The garden was a
watershed where gold and precious stones could also be found.

In the midst of this garden were two special trees, extraordinary
in fact. They were: (1) The tree of life and (2) The tree of the knowledge of good and evil. What was the difference between these
two special tress? It was the difference between immortality and
death. The tree of life, when partaken of, produced immortality,
and the tree of the knowledge of good and evil, when partaken
of, produced death.

God issued a stern warning to Adam not to eat of the latter tree,
because if and when he did, he would *"surely die"* (Genesis 2:17).

Unfortunately, Adam disobeyed, and death came upon him and, through him, upon the rest of mankind.

Was Adam aware of the other tree in the midst of the Garden of Eden, which was the tree of life? I believe he was. Why? Because God had said to him, *"Of every tree of the garden you may freely eat"* (Genesis 2:16), and that included the tree of life. But did Adam know about the beneficial effects of eating from the tree of life? I don't think so. Why did he not know this? Apparently he had not been informed by God about the extraordinary benefits of eating from the tree of life.

Why didn't God tell Adam about the benefits of eating from the tree of life, when He told him about the consequences of eating from the other tree? We can only theorize or conjecture. My guess is that God had probably planned to inform Adam about the benefits of the tree of life after he had passed the test. It seems apparent that Adam was on probation during this time. Otherwise, why would God have placed the tree of life in the midst of the Garden of Eden?

After Adam sinned, God immediately and with urgency placed Cherubims (a special order of angels) to guard the tree of life with a flaming sword. God's concern was that Adam might eat of the tree of life and *"live forever"* (Genesis 2:22). Since that time, the tree of life has not been found, but it reappeared in Heaven, according to the book of Revelation.

I am really intrigued, fascinated and mystified by this other tree, the tree of life. Was this a spiritual tree or perhaps a divine tree? God surely has lots of surprises in store for those of us who believe in His Son Jesus Christ. Jesus has promised all believers:

> *To him who overcomes I will give to eat from the tree of life, which*
> *is in the midst of the Paradise of God.*   Revelation 2:7

What a great promise!

THE RELEVANCE AND REALITY OF ANGELS

So He drove out the man; and He placed cherubim at the east of the garden of Eden, and a flaming sword which turned every way, to guard the way to the tree of life.   Genesis 3:24

But to which of the angels has He ever said:

"Sit at My right hand,
Till I make Your enemies Your footstool"?
Are they not all ministering spirits sent forth to minister for those who will inherit salvation?   Hebrews 1:13-14

Throughout the Bible, from the book of Genesis to the book of Revelation, we see the active involvement of angels in the affairs of God and man. We first see these heavenly beings in the Garden of Eden, standing guard with a flaming sword. They were tasked to preclude Adam and Eve from the tree of life after man had sinned against God.

Who or what are angels? We know very little about the origin of these heavenly beings. The Bible, however, does reveal that angels were also created and that they are spirit beings. They already existed before the Earth was created. Sometimes they were referred to as *"son[s] of the morning"* (Isaiah 14:12) or *"sons of God"* (Job 1:6, 2:1 and 38:7). They were created immortal, and therefore they cannot die. They are superior, compared with man, in terms of power and intelligence, but they are not all-powerful, and they are not omniscient.

At one time, an angel of the Lord massacred 185,000 Assyrian soldiers in one night. That's how powerful an angel is, so don't mess with them. They are also innumerable.

There are orders and ranks of angels according to the Bible. There are, for instance, the seraphim, the cherubim and the four living creatures. The main duty of these three orders of angels is to proclaim the holiness and the glory of God. They are constantly praising God around His throne. These are winged angels, but not all angels are winged. Some angels even appear in human form. There are the archangels — Michael and Gabriel — and the rest of the angels are guardian, guiding and protecting beings.

Angels were active participants before and during the birth of Christ. They announced the Good News of His birth first to Mary and, later, to the shepherds. An angel appeared to Joseph in a dream, clarifying some issues about Mary and warned Joseph of the impending danger to the child Jesus from the plotting of Herod, the current king.

Multitudes of angels came down from Heaven and sang praises to God at the birth of Jesus. Angels came and ministered to Jesus after His severe temptation in the wilderness. Thousands of angels were at the disposition of Jesus if He wanted to escape the death on the cross, but He did not.

The first herald of Jesus' resurrection was an angel as well, and angels proclaimed the return of Jesus to the disciples who were looking up as He was taken into Heaven.

Besides our protection and guidance, angels are also interested in the salvation of the lost. In fact, they rejoice when a soul gets saved.

I believe that every follower of Christ, being an *"heir of salvation,"* has a guardian angel dispatched by God to keep watch over them. This is good news! More good news is that God will elevate all followers of Christ at the resurrection to be *"as the angels"* in Heaven (Mark 12:25)!

In these dangerous times, security is a paramount concern for people the world over. We, as followers of Christ, need not worry because we have angels to guard us. Some years ago, I had a car accident while on my way up to Baguio City. [3] My car sustained serious damage in the accident, and it was thrown to the other side of the road. Miraculously, in all of this, I was unhurt. I believe that my guardian angel protected me. Praise God!

Can anyone avail themselves of a guardian angel? No, guardian angels are exclusively dispatched and assigned to those who are the *"heirs of salvation."* How can a person become an heir of salvation? It is easy, but it is also hard. Repent of your sins and receive Jesus Christ as your Lord and Savior. Then, live for God and follow Christ, and you will become an heir of salvation.

---

3. For those who are not familiar with Baguio City, it is the largest city in Northern Luzon, it sits high in the mountains, and the road leading there is winding and can be treacherous. The population of this once small mountain town has now soared to over 300,000.

THE SIGNIFICANCE OF TEN RIGHTEOUS

Then the LORD appeared to him [Abraham] by the terebinth trees of Mamre, as he was sitting in the tent door in the heat of the day. So he lifted his eyes and looked, and behold, three men were standing by him; and when he saw them, he ran from the tent door to meet them, and bowed himself to the ground, and said, "My Lord, if I have now found favor in Your sight, do not pass on by Your servant. Please let a little water be brought, and wash your feet, and rest yourselves under the tree. And I will bring a morsel of bread, that you may refresh your hearts. After that you may pass by, inasmuch as you have come to your servant." They said, "Do as you have said."   Genesis 18:1-5

One of the theophanies [4] in the Old Testament occurred when Abraham invited three persons to visit with him in his tent. These three visitors were no ordinary beings. Two of them were angels, and the third was the Lord Himself. Many theologians believe that He was the pre-incarnate Christ.

That day the Lord brought Abraham two pieces of news. The first one was good news, and the second one was bad news. The

---

4. A visible appearance of God, usually in human form

good news was that Sarah, Abraham's wife, would bear him a child, even though she was past the childbearing age. This would be a miracle. The second bit of news concerned the imminent destruction of Sodom and Gomorrah, together with the cities of the plains, because of their exceeding wickedness.

It is interesting to note that a sovereign God would reveal His plans ahead of time to one of His created beings such as Abraham. It was a great honor and privilege for Abraham, that God Almighty would disclose to him His will. But, then, Abraham was a special person in the eyes of God. He was, in fact, *"the Friend of God"* (James 2:23).

While the two angels proceeded to Sodom and Gomorrah to execute the judgment of God upon those cities, the Lord remained with Abraham. Knowing that his nephew Lot and his family were in the city of Sodom, Abraham began to intercede for Lot through an extraordinary and remarkable prayer. In approaching God on this subject, Abraham began with a question:

> *Would You also destroy the righteous with the wicked? Suppose there were fifty righteous within the city; would You also destroy the place and not spare it for the fifty righteous that were in it?*
> Genesis 18:23-24

God answered:

> *If I find in Sodom fifty righteous within the city, then I will spare all the place for their sakes.* Genesis 18:25

Abraham now apologized for his boldness, but he had to ask a similar question? Suppose there were forty-five righteous in the city. Would God still destroy it? God answered:

THE SIGNIFICANCE OF TEN RIGHTEOUS

If I find there forty-five, I will not destroy it. Genesis 18:28

But Abraham was not satisfied. He felt compelled to ask about forty, about thirty, about twenty and then about ten. God was consistent with His answers to this passionate prayer of Abraham. He would not destroy Sodom and Gomorrah for the sake of forty righteous, or thirty, or twenty or even ten. Unfortunately, Abraham stopped interceding at that point, and apparently there were not even ten righteous people to be found in all of Sodom and Gomorrah, and because of it, those cities were destroyed.

How unbelievable that out of the thousands of inhabitants of Sodom and Gomorrah, together with the cities of the plain, there was to be found only one righteous person, and that person was Abraham's nephew Lot. If there had been even ten righteous people there, Sodom and Gomorrah would not have been obliterated.

This all teaches us a divine principle of judgment: God will not destroy the righteous with the wicked. That means that the whole world owes a lot to the Christians. Why? Because we are *"the salt [or preservative] of the earth"* (Matthew 5:3). If anyone alive values human life, it is the Christian. Christians build more hospitals and more schools than anyone else. They have more involvement in humanitarian aid than anyone else, and they are very much into the preservation of our environment. The world as a whole is ripe for divine judgment, but because of the Christians in it, this judgment is yet averted.

How can we become righteous? Will our own righteousness suffice? No, our own righteousness is not acceptable to God. It is *"like filthy rags"* (Isaiah 64:6). The only acceptable righteousness to God is to be found in Jesus Christ. That's why it is indispensable that we receive Jesus Christ as our Lord and Savior.

273

Before that, we must first repent of our sins and receive Jesus Christ into our hearts by faith. Then and only then can we become righteous. In Christ, righteousness is imputed to us. Praise God! Glory to His holy name!

WHEN GOD BECAME A MAN

In the beginning was the Word, and the Word was with God, and the Word was God. He was in the beginning with God. All things were made through Him, and without Him nothing was made that was made. In Him was life, and the life was the light of men. And the light shines in the darkness, and the darkness did not comprehend it.   John 1:1-5

This was the foreword to John's Gospel. He continued with this:

He was in the world, and the world was made through Him, and the world did not know Him. He came to His own, and His own did not receive Him. But as many as received Him, to them He gave the right to become children of God, to those who believe in His name: who were born, not of blood, nor of the will of the flesh, nor of the will of man, but of God.   John 1:10-13

If that was not wonderful enough, he added:

And the Word became flesh and dwelt among us, and we beheld His glory, the glory as of the only begotten of the Father, full of grace and truth.   John 1:14

This foreword to John's Gospel is a paraphrase of Genesis 1, the first chapter of the first book of the Bible. Notice the similarities between the first phrases of each of the two books. Moses [5] opened his book with the words *"in the beginning"* (Genesis 1:1), and John opened his gospel with the same words.

Moses continued, *"In the beginning God"* and, in the same way, John wrote, *"In the beginning was the Word."* Both God and the Word were *"in the beginning,"* according to Moses and John.

John added that *"the Word was God"* and that He was *"with God"* in the beginning. There is no doubt that he was referring to Jesus as the Word and was showing us that He was and is God. As proof of this fact, John referred to Jesus as the One who created the world: *"All things were made through Him [Jesus], and without Him [Jesus] nothing was made that was made."*

Just as Genesis was the book of beginnings of the Old Testament, the Gospel of John is the book of beginnings for the New Testament, the beginnings of the life and ministry of Jesus Christ, the Son of God sent to redeem mankind.

It is also interesting to note that in Genesis 1:2, after God created the heavens and the earth, the earth was *"formless and empty,"* and *"darkness was over the surface of the deep"* (NIV). Some Bible scholars believe that between verses 1 and 2 a cataclysmic event occurred that rendered the earth empty and in darkness. They speculate that the earth had once been inhabited by angels who rebelled against God, and that this rebellion resulted in the destruction, emptiness and darkness of the earth.[6] These scholars may be speculating, but they have several biblical references to back up their theory. If they are right, then what Genesis 1:3 relays is actually a re-creation of the earth, not the original creation.

---

5. Most Bible scholars agree that Moses was the author of the book of Genesis.
6. Could this have been the time when dinosaurs and other giant animals roamed the earth?

Both Moses and John mention light:

And God said, "Let there be light," and there was light.

Genesis 1:3, NIV

John also mentioned the light, but he said that Jesus Christ is the light of men and that He shines in darkness.

Now, several questions must be asked: How did God become a man? Why did God become a man? Where did this happen? And when did this happen?

Maybe it would be logical to start with the second question: Why did God become a man? I can think of at least two reasons given by the Bible. The first is that He did it to save mankind from sin and destruction:

For God so loved the world that he gave his one and only Son, that whoever believes in him shall not perish but have eternal life. For God did not send his Son into the world to condemn the world, but to save the world through him. Whoever believes in him is not condemned, but whoever does not believe stands condemned already because they have not believed in the name of God's one and only Son. John 3:16-18

The second reason, I believe, why God became a man was to show people everywhere who He was. Before He became a man, people didn't know the one true and living God. They worshipped many different gods, even unknown gods. This is one reason why there are so many different religions in the world. In Jesus Christ, we see, know and understand the true and living God, because He is God. He is *"the express image"* of the invisible God (Hebrews 1:3). Besides the other innumerable witnesses and His own words and miraculous works, God the Father Himself affirmed the deity of Jesus.

How did God become a man? The Bible says, *"The Word became flesh and made His dwelling among us"* (NIV). The modern word for this miracle is *incarnation*. Mary was instrumental in this divine process. This is the doctrine that the eternal Son of God became human and that He did so without, in any manner or degree, diminishing His divine nature.

This divine condescension is also relative to the other questions I mentioned: Where and when did this happen? It happened in a little town called Bethlehem (where King David was from). Joseph had taken Mary and gone to Bethlehem to register for the census because he was of the lineage of David. While they were there, Jesus was born. They had found lodging in a stable, and now Mary wrapped the baby Jesus in cloths and placed Him in a manger.

This momentous and historical event happened this way because Caesar Augustus had issued a decree that a census should be taken of the entire Roman world, and everyone was sent to their hometown to register. Was it just a coincidence? Definitely not. It was divine providence.

That God became man is the basis of the Christmas story. Christ, the Son of God, was born in Bethlehem of Judea, and His birth was welcomed by multitudes of angelic hosts, who all sang in jubilation:

> *Glory to God in the highest,*
> *And on earth peace, goodwill toward men!*   Luke 2:14

Unfortunately, only a handful of people welcomed Jesus' birth. These were led by Mary and Joseph and the shepherds, but they also included some of those who heard the news the shepherds offered. Most of those who heard about His birth were indifferent, but not the shepherds:

Then the shepherds returned, glorifying and praising God for all the things that they had heard and seen, as it was told them.
                                                            Luke 2:20

At Christmas time and every day of the year, let us welcome Jesus Christ by receiving Him into our hearts, our homes, our churches and our communities with joy and gladness, just like Mary, Joseph and the shepherds did that first Christmas day. Let Christ's birth be the center and the focus of our Christmas celebrations and our daily walk. Let us know and understand the significance and the true meaning of God becoming a man. In this way, we will have a truly blessed and merry Christmas and can count on a happy and prosperous New Year to come — every year.

WHEN GOD GAVE UP

Therefore God also gave them up to uncleanness, in the lusts of their hearts, to dishonor their bodies among themselves, who exchanged the truth of God for the lie, and worshiped and served the creature rather than the Creator, who is blessed forever. Amen. For this reason God gave them up to vile passions.

... they which commit such things are worthy of death.

Romans 1:24-26 and 32

Does God run out of patience with sinful and wicked people? Yes, it is apparent that He does. In this passage, such people are clearly warned of the impending wrath of God from Heaven.

Look at it again:

God gave them up.   Verse 24

God gave them up.   Verse 26

This phrase *"god gave them up"* is used twice in quick succession in this first chapter of Romans. This suggests a seriousness and a

280

heartfelt concern with regards to the judgment to be visited upon rebellious people, whether individually or as a nation. God said:

Because I have called and you refused,
I have stretched out my hand and no one regarded,
Because you disdained all my counsel,
And would have none of my rebuke,
I also will laugh at your calamity;
I will mock when your terror comes,
When your terror comes like a storm,
And your destruction comes like a whirlwind,
When distress and anguish come upon you.
Then they will call on me, but I will not answer;
They will seek me diligently, but they will not find me.
Because they hated knowledge
And did not choose the fear of the LORD,
They would have none of my counsel
And despised my every rebuke.
Therefore they shall eat the fruit of their own way,
And be filled to the full with their own fancies.
For the turning away of the simple will slay them,
And the complacency of fools will destroy them;
But whoever listens to me will dwell safely,
And will be secure, without fear of evil.   Proverbs 1:24-33

There are two specific sins which are foremost among the causes of God's pronouncement of judgment upon certain people: idolatry and sexual immorality. Other sins are mentioned, like murder, covetousness, disobedience to parents, wickedness, hatred of God, lawbreaking, boastfulness and the lack of mercy, but two are shown to be of the utmost importance.

What is idolatry? It is worshipping something created rather than the Creator Himself. This is a violation of the second commandment concerning the making and worshipping of images. This religious practice was prevalent from the time of Abraham on down through the Old Testament and then into New Testament times. The Greeks and Romans were idolaters, and the early Church was contaminated with their idolatry after Christianity was declared the state religion of the Roman Empire. Ever since then, many have been blinded to idolatrous worship, which God detests and abhors.

What is sexual immorality? It is the promiscuous practice and relationships between two persons of the same sex. Other names for it are sodomy and homosexuality. Whereas, in the old days, to be gay was "taboo," nowadays, it is an accepted norm. Gays are now proud to proclaim to the world that they are gay and that "gay is okay." No matter what justifications or arguments these people might put forward, in the sight of God it is not okay. According to many medical experts, the proliferation of the deadly disease known as AIDS [Auto Immune Deficiency Syndrome] is the consequence of this unnatural sexual practice. AIDS leaves a Sword of Damocles hanging over the heads of those who practice unnatural sex.

What was the effect when God gave these people up to a reprobate mind? The destruction of the inhabitants of Sodom and Gomorrah is one very good Bible answer. Despite the intercessory prayers of the righteous Abraham, the wickedness of the people was so overwhelming that finally God decided to annihilate them with fire and brimstone from Heaven.

Is that scarey? Yes, it certainly is! Is there a remedy? Yes! Can God reverse His impending judgment? Yes! The case of the people of Nineveh in the Old Testament is a very good example. God sent

His prophet Jonah to announce impending doom to the people of Nineveh because of their wickedness. The result was that from the greatest to the least, the people of Nineveh believed God and repented, and God spared them from judgment.

God is *"no respecter of persons"* (Acts 10:34, KJV), and He is *"the same yesterday, today and forever"* (Hebrews 13:8). If you are willing to repent and turn from your wicked ways, you can save yourself from the wrath of God to come. Open your heart in prayer and receive Jesus Christ as your personal Lord and Savior and you will be saved. Then follow God and live for Him the rest of your life.

WHO WERE THE WISE MEN OF CHRISTMAS?

Now after Jesus was born in Bethlehem of Judea in the days of Herod the king, behold, wise men from the East came to Jerusalem, saying, "Where is He who has been born King of the Jews? For we have seen His star in the East and have come to worship Him." Matthew 2:1-2

Several mysterious men called *magi* or *wise men* came to Jerusalem looking for Jesus. The circumstances surrounding them and their visit have been shrouded in controversy ever since. Who were they? And where were they from?

One of our traditional Christmas carols says:

We three kings of Orient are;
Bearing gifts we traverse afar,
Field and fountain, moor and mountain,
Following yonder star. [7]

Were these visitors really kings? Were there really three of them? Were they really riding on camels, as they have been depicted in many popular artistic conceptions? Were they really from the

---

7. John Henry Hopkins, Jr., 1857

Orient? There are many things yet to be clarified concerning these mysterious guests.

First, the Bible does not call them kings, but, rather, magi or wise men. Next, there were probably more than three of them. In those days it was very dangerous to travel in small groups, especially that far because thieves waited along the known travel routes to steal anything they could. So these men were probably part of a brigade of magi.

Were they riding camels? Probably not. Something about the wise men caused Herod and the people of Jerusalem to fear, so some have wondered if they might not have been mounted on powerful steeds outfitted for war.

Matthew described the wise men as having come from *"the east,"* not necessarily from the Orient.

Several places in the Bible speak of wise men. The first was during the time of Joseph, when Pharaoh, the king of Egypt, had a dream and was troubled about the dream. When he woke up, he sent for men he thought might be able to explain his dream:

> *Now it came to pass in the morning that his spirit was troubled, and he sent and called for all the magicians of Egypt and all its wise men. And Pharaoh told them his dreams, but there was no one who could interpret them for Pharaoh.* Genesis 41:8

Pharaoh told these respected men his dreams, but not one of them was able to interpret it. This was what led to Joseph being called from the prison, and with wisdom and favour from God, he was able to interpret the dream.

The second mention of wise men was during the time of Moses. This also took place in Pharaoh's court, but it was a different time and a different Pharaoh. When Aaron, Moses' brother, threw

285

his staff in front of Pharaoh and it became a snake, Pharaoh then summoned men called wise men, sorcerers and magicians, and they seemingly were able to do the same thing by their magic arts:

> But Pharaoh also called the wise men and the sorcerers; so the magicians of Egypt, they also did in like manner with their enchantments. For every man threw down his rod, and they became serpents. But Aaron's rod swallowed up their rods. And Pharaoh's heart grew hard, and he did not heed them, as the LORD had said.   Exodus 7:11-13

The third mention of wise men also involved a dream. This time it was King Nebuchadnezzar of Babylon who had dreamed, and again he was troubled by his dreams and could no longer sleep. Like the Pharaoh before him, King Nebuchadnezzar summoned men whom he thought might be able to help him interpret his dreams. The problem was that he had forgotten the dreams, so now he expected them to first tell him the dreams and then tell him the interpretation:

> Then the king gave the command to call the magicians, the astrologers, the sorcerers, and the Chaldeans to tell the king his dreams.   Daniel 2:2

Here, for the first time, we can see a possible connection to our magi of Matthew 2. These men were learned and prominent. They were employed at the King's court, possibly as advisers or consultants to the king. Many historians suggest that although these men were not kings themselves, they were almost certainly kingmakers. One of them was named Daniel, and he was a Jewish exile in the land.

During the Babylonian captivity of the Jews, sometime around 586 B.C., Daniel was found among those who had been carried away captive into Babylon. By Providence, he was chosen and trained as a member of this group of magi, due to the exceptional talents God had given him. He could understand visions and dreams of all kinds, and when examined, he was found *"ten times better"* than all the magicians and enchanters in the whole of the kingdom (Daniel 1:20).

When the first group of magicians and astrologers called were unable to tell the king his dreams and their interpretation, he was so furious that he ordered the execution of all the wise men in Babylon. The decree of death which was issued as a result included Daniel and his friends.

When Daniel received this notice, he quickly went to the palace to ask the king for a little more time. He then returned home and told his friends what was happening, and they all began to pray for wisdom. The clock was ticking.

After prayer, Daniel was very confident:

> *Then Daniel went to Arioch, whom the king had appointed to execute the wise men of Babylon, and said to him, "Do not execute the wise men of Babylon. Take me to the king, and I will interpret his dream for him."*
> Daniel 2:24

That confidence was not misplaced. Daniel was indeed able to interpret the king's dreams. In doing this, Daniel was able, not only to save himself and his friends, but also all of the wise men of the land.

Because Daniel saved these men from certain death, I believe he was given the opportunity to share with them his faith in God, and many were converted. There is also no doubt in my mind that

Daniel told them about the prophecies concerning the coming Messiah. Because of their Daniel connection, these magi or wise men embraced the God of Daniel.

It seems apparent to me that the magi or wise men who came to Jerusalem seeking the newborn King of the Jews were descendants of the group of people whom Daniel had converted to his Jewish faith. How else could these Magi know about the birth of the Messiah, unless someone had told them this information? Daniel was the link. He gave them this information.

What about the star that the wise men saw in the east and that guided them until it rested over the place where the infant Jesus was? Was it a heavenly body as many suggest? I don't believe that this star was a heavenly body, otherwise the place where it rested would have burned. I believe that this star was the glory of Jesus, which He temporarily relinquished. This is what the Magi saw in the east, and it guided them to the place where the infant Jesus was.

If we look a map of the land in those days and trace back to where the magi might have come from, *"the east"* was just about where present-day Iraq is located. That is also where ancient Babylon was located, so it was a logical base for our Daniel connection.

The magi of Matthew 2, after finding Jesus and fulfilling their mission of worshipping Him and giving Him their gifts, returned to their own country with new faith in the Lord. This explains why there are many Christians in Iraq. I believe that the Christians there are descendants of the magi who found the baby Jesus in Bethlehem of Judea.

Oh, how amazing and wonderful are the grace and mercy of God! This group of people, who were of the priestly caste of the Medes and who practiced astrology, divination, sorcery and magic, were once detestable in the sight of God. In fact, God warned and precluded the Israelites from involving themselves in any of these detestable practices when they entered Canaan. But through the Daniel connection, these magi became the first gentile witness of Christmas and eventually became the first gentile converts to Christianity.

The big challenge for us Christians today, relative to this Christmas episode, is to be more like Daniel. Let us be bold in our witness for Christ and share our faith in God with unbelievers wherever and whenever we have the opportunity. Jesus said:

> *But you will receive power when the Holy Spirit comes on you; and you will be my witnesses in Jerusalem, and in all Judea and Samaria, and to the ends of the earth.* Acts 1:8

Amen!

WHY DO BAD THINGS HAPPEN TO GOOD AND GODLY PEOPLE?

The steps of a good man are ordered by the LORD,
And He delights in his way.
Though he fall, he shall not be utterly cast down;
For the LORD upholds him with His hand.   Psalm 37:23-24

There is a saying: "If there is an effect, then there must be a cause." This can be expressed conversely: "With every cause, there is an effect." Are there always causes to the bad things that happen to good and godly people? Maybe if those same bad things happened to bad people, we might not question them. We might even concur with many that bad things happen to bad people as a consequence of their bad behavior. Why? And what are the causes of the bad things that happen to good and godly people? To find the answer to these questions, let us look at examples of good and godly people in the Bible who experienced bad things in their lives.

First, let us look at Samson in the book of Judges. Samson was a good man. As a matter of fact, he was extraordinarily gifted. When the Spirit of God came upon him, he had superhuman strength. With this strength, he became a deliverer of his people, the Israelites, against the oppression and affliction of their enemies, the Philistines. At one time, Samson killed a thousand Philistines using only the jawbone of a donkey. But some bad things also happened to Samson, despite his previous victories against his enemies. Eventually he suffered defeat and humiliation at their hands, and his life ended in tragedy. Why?

The causes of the bad things that happened to Samson are not hard to find. He unwisely involved himself with bad women, and those bad women were from among his enemies, the Philistines. The greater reason was that the Lord had left him, and Samson failed to recognize that fact until it was too late.

Another example was David. He was a good man and one of God's favorite people. In fact, he was dubbed: *"a man after his [God's] own heart"* (1 Samuel 13:14). David taught us much about worship and left us his powerful psalms as an example to follow. In one of those many powerful psalms, he sang those words: *"The steps of a good man are ordered by the LORD, and He delights in his way."* Unfortunately, bad things happened to David and his family. His son Absalom rebelled against him and was killed. Including Absalom, four of David's children died tragic deaths.

David also suffered terrible shame and scandal. Why? What was the cause? The answer is not hard to find. He had no business engaging in an adulterous relationship with a married woman named Bathsheba. He got so obsessed with this woman that he hatched a sinister plot to murder her husband, and that plot was carried out. It goes without saying that these things strongly displeased the Lord.

On the other hand, Daniel had some friends who escaped the effects of the bad things that seemed destined to destroy them. Their names were Shadrach, Meshach and Abednego, and they were also among the Jewish exiles in Babylon.

The king made a decree that everyone must bow down and worship the golden image he had set up, and anyone who refused would be instantly thrown into a blazing furnace. For their part, these three men decided not to obey, and when the time came to bow down, they refused. When they were drug before the king, and he reminded them of the consequences of their actions, they responded:

> *O Nebuchadnezzar, we have no need to answer you in this matter. If that is the case, our God whom we serve is able to deliver us from the burning fiery furnace, and He will deliver us from your hand, O king. But if not, let it be known to you, O king, that we do not serve your gods, nor will we worship the gold image which you have set up.*   Daniel 3:16-18

Nebuchadnezzar was furious with such insolence, and he ordered the furnace to be heated seven times hotter than usual. Then he commanded the strongest of his soldiers to tie these three men up and throw them into the blazing furnace. The fire was so intense that even the soldiers who took up Meshach, Shadrach and Abednego were killed.

When the three fell into the blazing furnace, the king leaped to his feet in amazement at what he saw before him and asked:

> *Did we not cast three men bound into the midst of the fire?... Look! ... I see four men loose, walking in the midst of the fire; and they are not hurt, and the form of the fourth is like the Son of God.*   Daniel 3:24-25

Those three Hebrew young men came out of the fire, and the king's officer saw that the fire had not harmed their bodies Their hair and clothes had no smell of fire on them. In this ways, God was glorified, and the king declared that no one in his kingdom would be allowed to speak a word against the God of Meshach, Shadrach and Abednego, who were then promoted.

Another example of this effect was Daniel himself. When King Darius promoted Daniel to the top position in the kingdom, other officials became jealous of him. They tried to find any charge or accusation of corruption or negligence against him they could make, but could not, because he was so trustworthy. So they devised a scheme and persuaded the king to issue an edict that anyone who prayed to any god besides the king would be thrown into a lions' den.

Daniel was not intimidated by the king's decree, and he remained resolute in his faith in God — the true God, the God of Israel. As was his regular practice, he got down on his knees and prayed, giving thanks to God every day in his house.

Soon Daniel's enemies went to the king and told him that Daniel was violating his decree. Although the king was hesitant, he ordered that Daniel be thrown into the lions' den. Because he knew Daniel, he expected God to help him. He said to Daniel:

Your God, whom you serve continually, He will deliver you.
Daniel 6:16

That night the king was restless and could not sleep. Early the next morning, he hurriedly went to the lions' den. When he came near the entrance, he called out to Daniel in an anguished voice:

Daniel, servant of the living God, has your God, whom you serve continually, been able to deliver you from the lions?
Daniel 6:20

He was relieved to hear Daniel answer:

O king, live forever! My God sent His angel and shut the lions'
mouths, so that they have not hurt me, because I was found in-
nocent before Him; and also, O king, I have done no wrong before
you.   Daniel 6:21-22

When Daniel was lifted out of the lions' den, no wound was found on him. He had trusted in His God, and God had protected him.

So what are the causes and effects of why bad things happen to good and godly people? In our first two examples of people who experienced bad things in their lives, we found that the causes of the bad things originated from their own bad behavior, and the effects of those bad things on them was suffering. So, these were self-invited troubles. On the other hand, in the last two examples, the bad things that happened did not originate from their own bad behavior, but the behavior of bad people. When it happened, they did not compromise their faith, so God protected them from harm, and they did not suffer.

Always remember:

Do not be deceived, God is not mocked; for whatever a man sows,
that he will also reap.   Galatians 6:7

I believe that the Lord's promise, *"Lo, I will be with you always"* (Matthew 28:20), is not absolute. Two Christians were in a car, and the driver was driving too fast. The passenger said, "Brother, I think you're driving too fast!"

The driver answered, "Don't worry! The Lord is with us."

"You're wrong," the other man answered. "He left when you exceeded the speed limit!" So keep safe by staying away from troubles:

Abhor what is evil. Cling to what is good. Romans 12:9

Amen!

#UNSELFIE

I have been crucified with Christ and I no longer live, but Christ lives in me. The life I now live in the body, I live by faith in the Son of God, who loved me and gave himself for me.

Galatians 2:20

The theme of our Star of Hope Philippines 2015 Youth Camp was *#Unselfie*. What is *#Unselfie*? When I looked for the word *unselfie* or the root word *selfie* in the dictionary, I could not find either one. When I looked for *hash tag*, I also did not find that term. I guess my dictionary is outdated. The English language is constantly changing.

It is amazing nowadays to see the advances in technology. A smart phone in the palm of your hand can provide you with many things, including advanced information on the development of new words in English. Through Google and Wikipedia I found that *selfie*, the root word of *unselfie*, is defined as "a continual taking of one's image or photo by means of a digital camera or smart phone and posting those photos on social media like Facebook."

Now, there are questions relative to this modern trend among Christians, especially our young people. It seems that the word *unselfie* suggests that such a practice is contrary to our Christian and moral convictions. Is it unchristian or immoral to take a *selfie*? I honestly believe that there is nothing basically unchristian or immoral about the *selfie* trend. However, I believe that it is wrong for Christians to place within their own social account the photos of other people, especially those of movie stars or fashion models, just to be associated with beautiful people. This is identity theft, it is stealing, and it is wrong!

Another thing I don't like is this: Why do people make themselves ugly by posting their disfigured faces? Paul wrote to the Galatians that he no longer lived, but now Christ lived in him. Let the image people get from us be wholesome and Christlike.

The term *selfie* may have a spiritual significance. In this sense, the practice of the *selfie* is nothing new. It was practiced in Heaven long ago. One of the archangels by the name of Lucifer, also known as Satan or the devil, took the original *selfie*. He declared:

> *I will ascend into heaven,*
> *I will exalt my throne above the stars of God;*
> *I will also sit on the mount of the congregation*
> *On the farthest sides of the north.*
> *I will ascend above the heights of the clouds,*
> *I will be like the Most High.*　　　　　Isaiah 14:13-14

But Satan was brought down — big time.

Back in the Garden of Eden, Satan disguised himself as a serpent, and then he beguiled and deceived Eve to do a *selfie*, and man fell into sin. And that was the beginning of human misery and death, so that the Old Testament ended in the word *curse*. But Jesus came to remedy that curse:

For God so loved the world [humanity] that He gave His only begotten Son, that whoever believes in Him should not perish but have everlasting life. John 3:16

God gave His Son Jesus to save us, so that Jesus Christ became the King of the UNSELFIE! Look at this:

Let this mind be in you which was also in Christ Jesus, who, being in the form of God, did not consider it robbery to be equal with God, but made Himself of no reputation, taking the form of a bondservant, and coming in the likeness of men. And being found in appearance as a man, He humbled Himself and became obedient to the point of death, even the death of the cross. Therefore God also has highly exalted Him and given Him the name which is above every name, that at the name of Jesus every knee should bow, of those in heaven, and of those on earth, and of those under the earth, and that every tongue should confess that Jesus Christ is Lord, to the glory of God the Father. Philippians 2:5-11

The big challenge for everyone now is this: How can he or she *unselfie* himself or herself. The answer can be found in the testimony of St. Paul: *"I no longer live, but Christ lives in me."* He added: *"I live by faith in the Son of God, who loved me and gave himself for me."*

How can we receive such a spiritually *UNSELFIE* life? The Bible tells us to repent of our sins and believe the Gospel. It tells us to humble ourselves in the sight of God, open our hearts, and invite Jesus Christ to come in as our personal Lord and Savior. If we do this, we will saved. Then, find a good Bible-believing church, fellowship with God's people, and grow in the grace of our Lord Jesus Christ. Amen!

WHEN ALL THINGS ARE ALMOST LOST

There was a man in the land of Uz, whose name was Job; and that man was blameless and upright, and one who feared God and shunned evil.   Job 1:1

Mishaps and misfortunes that bring devastation and misery to mankind are beyond our control. These include hurricanes, tornados, earthquakes, tsunamis, fires and floods. It is a painful experience when you encounter a survivor of one of these events who has been stripped of everything he once owned, or has even lost his entire family, when he has done nothing wrong. It all happened because he was struck by some calamity or catastrophe and has experienced its terrible destruction. In these situations, many lose hope and commit suicide. As Christians, how should we respond to such an occurrence?

Perhaps a fire gutted your home or even killed some or all of your family members. Perhaps the company you worked for shut down, and you suddenly lost your source of income, putting your whole family at risk. What are we to do when everything seems lost? Who can we go to? Who can we call?

The Old Testament story of Job is a great comfort to anyone suffering unjustly. It can inspire and challenge those who face any adverse and unpleasant situations in life.

So that we can understand Job's situation better, the terrible trials and tests he endured, and how he overcame them, let us acquaint ourselves with the cast of characters in this human/divine drama. Job, of course, is the main character. Then, there was God Himself, followed by Satan, and Job's wife and children, his friends, his servants and his enemies — the Sabeans and Chaldeans. The settings for these events were: (1) The land of Uz and (2) Heaven.

As the first act of this drama opens, Job is described by the narrator as a man of moral integrity. He was upright and blameless. He feared God and shunned evil. Job was also extremely wealthy and was considered to be the greatest man among all the people of the east.

Then the narrator shifts his focus to a heavenly scene, where the angels have come together to present themselves before the Lord. Interestingly enough, Satan is there along with them.

The Lord asks Satan, *"From where do you come?"* (Job 1:7).

Satan answers, *"From going to and fro on the earth, and from walking back and forth on it"* (same verse).

Then the Lord says to Satan, *"Have you considered My servant Job, that there is none like him on the earth, a blameless and upright man, one who fears God and shuns evil?"* (Job 1:8).

Satan is not so sure and asks, *"Does Job fear God for nothing?"* He goes on to argue: "You protected him and his family and blessed his work so that his flocks became numerous. But strike everything he has, and he will surely curse you" (see Job 1:10-11).

Amazingly, the Lord answers Satan, "Very well, then, everything he has is in your hands, but don't touch him personally" (see verse 12).

Back on Earth, Satan unleashes his destructive power against Job, and through his influence on human and natural elements, deals Job's livestock devastating blows. Job not only loses them all (and they represented his ability to provide for himself), but that same day all of his children are killed. How unlucky can one man be? Surprisingly, instead of cursing God, Job worships and praises Him (see verses 20-22).

Back in Heaven again, God repeats His praise of Job's moral integrity before Satan, and Satan insists, "Strike his flesh and bones and he will surely curse you" (see Job 2:4-5). Again the Lord allows Satan to afflict Job, this time with painful sores throughout his body, but God precludes Satan from killing His servant.

Job is in pain now, in such a miserable condition that his wife joins the pressure for him to curse God. His friends come along, and they express their empathy for a while, but in the end, they become *"miserable comforters"* (Job 16:2). What a terrible blow! Job is now experiencing extreme pressure.

You and I, as readers of this story, are only passive participants and as such, are privileged to see the broader picture and the greater perspective of it all. It is clear that Job's understanding of all these bad circumstances and situations that have befallen him came from God. He said:

> *The LORD gave, and the LORD has taken away;*
> *Blessed be the name of the LORD.*   Job 1:21

I agree with him fully on the first part, *"The LORD gave."* I do not agree with the second part: *"The Lord has taken away."* Clearly it was not God who took everything away from Job; it was Satan. It was not God who afflicted Job with sickness; it was Satan. Far too many people blame their misfortunes and sicknesses on God.

Even insurance companies, when wishing to excuse themselves of responsibility and not accept liability when things they have insured are destroyed by calamities, have a special clause in each contract that frees them of all responsibility for "Acts of God." Don't blame God for your misfortunes and bad circumstances; blame Satan instead.

Did Job know that it was Satan who brought all these situations into his life? I don't think so. Did he know that he was being used by God as a pawn in a game of chess between God and Satan? I don't think so. But as we read the story of Job, it becomes clear that it was Satan who caused all these troubles.

The statement of Jesus concerning Satan (who is also called the devil) is most appropriate in Job's situation. He said:

> *The thief [Satan] does not come except to steal, and to kill, and*
> *to destroy.* John 10:10

Job had no idea that bad things come from the devil. He assumed that everything — good or bad — comes from God. He even thought that God might kill him. He said:

> *Though he slay me, yet will I hope in him.* Job 13:15, NIV

Generally speaking, God does not kill people, and He certainly is not delighted when He sees anyone in desperate situations or in poverty. God is an advocate for life. He is a good God, who loves to bless His people and give them abundant life. That was the counterweight found in the rest of John 10:10:

> *I have come that they may have life, and that they may have it*
> *more abundantly.*

Jesus also said:

I am the way, the truth, and the life.   John 14:6

God is the very Giver of Life. In Him is life! Therefore it is wrong for Christians, when their loved ones have died, to say that the Lord has taken them. Whether Christian or not, people die because they are human and, thus, mortal.

If we, as Christians, become victims of disaster or calamity, can we say that those things were caused by the devil? If we get sick, can we say that it was the devil who made us sick? It is possible, especially if we are living faithfully for God. Sometimes, however, we have no one to blame but ourselves, especially in many cases of sickness. Before we became a Christian, we may have abused our bodies through various vices, like smoking cigarettes, excessive drinking or the use of illicit drugs. Now, with the passing of the years, our immune systems have weakened, so that sicknesses take hold. Always remember: What we sow we reap:

Do not be deceived, God is not mocked; for whatever a man sows, that he will also reap.   Galatians 6:7

This is true, even if we are now Christians.

Job finally emerged resilient and victorious over the terrible calamities he experienced in his life, and the Lord made him prosperous again and gave him twice as much as he'd had before:

Now the LORD blessed the latter days of Job more than his beginning; for he had fourteen thousand sheep, six thousand camels, one thousand yoke of oxen, and one thousand female donkeys. He also had seven sons and three daughters.   Job 42:12-13

Job went on to live 140 years and to enjoy four generations of descendants. How was he able to overcome his severe trials and testings? As we have seen, his theology was rather imperfect, but he loved God, and that was good enough for God to grant him total victory. In the end, what mattered was that Job was determined to trust God, come what may, and we can emulate him when similar situations arise in our lives.

Our Lord Jesus Christ is alive, and no calamity can change that fact. If we have accepted His as our Lord and Savior, He is with us — no matter what might come our way. Hallelujah!

HEAVEN, THE ABODE OF GOD

In the beginning God created the heaven and the earth.

Genesis 1:1

As Christians, we believe in Heaven. In fact, Heaven is one of the essential elements of our faith, and both the Old and New Testaments are replete with the subject. The Bible even opens with the statement that in the beginning God created Heaven and Earth.

As Christians, Heaven is our hope and ultimate destiny. We believe that those Christians who have already died will go to Heaven. We sing about Heaven in our worship services and are admonished in the Scriptures to ponder it.

For His part, Jesus said:

Do not lay up for yourselves treasures on earth, where moth and rust destroy and where thieves break in and steal; but lay up for yourselves treasures in heaven, where neither moth nor rust destroys and where thieves do not break in and steal. For where your treasure is, there your heart will be also.

Matthew 6:19-21

When the Bible refers to *"the heavens,"* the meaning is different. *Heaven* is one thing, and *the heavens* are something else entirely. There are three places referred to in the Scriptures as *heaven* or *heavens*. We might call them the first heaven, the second heaven and the third Heaven. The first heaven is the expanse and firmament surrounding the earth's atmosphere, where clouds are gathered. This was the area mentioned in the Old Testament when the people built a tower in Babel that they wanted to reached up to *"the heavens"* (Genesis 11:4). It was the first heaven that Enoch and Elijah were translated into, as well as Philip in the New Testament.

The second heaven is outer space, beyond the earth's atmosphere, where the other planets are located.

The third Heaven is the dwelling place of God. In his second letter to the Corinthian believers, Paul actually called it *"the third heaven"* (2 Corinthians 12:2).

Is Heaven real or just imaginary? Personally, I believe that Heaven is real. Just as the Earth that God created is real, so also is the Heaven that He created.

What is Heaven like? The Bible shows that Heaven is a paradise. It is a place of exquisite beauty and eternal bliss. It is a Garden of Eden. Jesus, while hanging on the cross of Calvary, promised the repentant malefactor that he would be with Him *"in paradise"* (Luke 23:43).

The Bible also calls Heaven *"a country"* (Hebrews 11:16). This means that Heaven has a defined territory, a population, a government and a sovereignty. Heaven is also likened to *"a city"* where there are lots of inhabitants and a rather complex and highly urbanized political subdivision (Revelation 21:10-). Finally, Heaven is *"a kingdom"* where there is a King and His subjects (Matthew 18:23-35). The Kingdom of Heaven is the same as the Kingdom of God.

Although no eye has seen, no ear has heard and no mind has conceived of what God has prepared for those who love Him, He has chosen to reveal it to us by His Spirit (see 1 Corinthians 2:9-10). The latter part of the Book of Revelation gives us a glimpse of the physical description of Heaven.

Someday the dwelling of God (Heaven) will be with His people, and God Himself will dwell among us (see Revelation 21:1-3). He will wipe away every tear from our eyes. There will be no more death or mourning or crying or pain, for the old order has passed away (see verse 4). The Holy City, the new Jerusalem, by allegory, describes Heaven as a city of pure gold which shines with the glory of God, and its brilliance is like that of a very precious jewel. The foundations of the City are made of precious stones (see verse 19), the gates are made of pearl (see verse 21), and the great street was of pure gold, like transparent glass (see verse 18).

There is the river flowing through Heaven which is the water of life, as clear as crystal, flowing from the throne of God and of the Lamb down the middle of the great street of the city (see Revelation 22:1). On each side of the river stand the tree of life, bearing twelve crops of fruit, yielding its fruit every month. And the leaves of the tree are for the healing of the nations (see verse 2). There will be no more curses.

The throne of God and of the Lamb will be in the city, and His servants will serve Him (see verse 22:3). They will see His face, and His name will be on their foreheads (see verse 4).

There will be no more night. They will not need the light of a lamp or the light of the sun, for the Lord God will give them light. And they will reign for ever and ever (see verse 5).

Who will not be allowed to enter Heaven? The answer is: those who are cowardly, the unbelieving, the vile, the murderers, the sexually immoral, those who practice magic arts, the idolaters, those who are impure, the deceitful and all liars (see Revelation 21:8).

Who will be allowed to enter Heaven? The answer is: only those whose names are written in the Lamb's book of life (see Revelation 21:27).

How can our names be written in the Lamb's book of life? We must repent of our sins, open our hearts and receive Jesus Christ into our life as our personal Lord and Savior. Then, God will give us the right to become His children. To those who believe in Him and follow Him, Jesus said:

> *In My Father's house are many mansions; if it were not so, I would have told you. I go to prepare a place for you. And if I go and prepare a place for you, I will come again and receive you to Myself; that where I am, there you may be also.*   John 14:2-3

What a promise! Hallelujah!

Amen!

A Short Glossary of Filipino Words Used

Nanay — Mother, Mom, Mama
Tatay — Father, Dad, Daddy
Lola — Grandmother, Grandma, Grandmamma
Lolo — Grandfather, Grandad, Granddaddy,
barrangay — formerly called *barrio*, the smallest administrative division in the Philippines and the native Filipino term for a village, district or ward. In colloquial usage, the term often refers to an inner city neighborhood, a suburb or a suburban neighborhood. [1]

---

1. http://en.wikipedia.org/wiki/Barangay

Author Contact Page

You may contact the author in the following ways:

Pastor Gani Coruña
P.O. Box 154 G.P.O.
Greenhills Commercial Center
Greenhills, San Juan City, 1502
Metro Manila
Philippines

E-Mail: gani.coruna@starofhope.org

www.ingramcontent.com/pod-product-compliance
Lightning Source LLC
LaVergne TN
LVHW051224080426
835513LV00016B/1390